Cram101 Textbook Outlines to accompany:

Discovering Hospitality and Tourism : Worlds Greatest Industry

Jack D. Ninemeier, 2nd Edition

A Content Technologies Inc. publication (c) 2011.

PRACTICE EXAMS.

Get all of the self-teaching practice exams for each chapter of this textbook at
www.Cram101.com and ace the tests. Here is an example:

Chapter 1

Discovering Hospitality and Tourism : Worlds Greatest Industry
Jack D. Ninemeier, 2nd Edition,
All Material Written and Prepared by Cram101

I WANT A BETTER GRADE.   Items 1 - 50 of 100. ▶

1 The _____ consists of companies within the food services, accommodations, recreation, and entertainment
sectors.

The _____ is a several billion dollar industry that mostly depends on the availability of leisure time and disposable
income. A hospitality unit such as a restaurant, hotel, or even an amusement park consists of multiple groups such as
facility maintenance, direct operations (servers, housekeepers, porters, kitchen workers, bartenders, etc).,
management, marketing, and human resources.

◯ Hospitality industry   ◯ H. Milton Stewart School of Industrial
                                      and Systems Engineering

◯ Haasrode Research-Park   ◯ Habanero

2 In the contexts of real estate and lodging, _____ are any tangible or intangible benefits of a property, especially
those which increase the attractiveness or value of the property or which contribute to its comfort or convenience.

Tangible _____ might include parks, swimming pools, health club facilities, party rooms, guest rooms (lodgings),
theater or media rooms, bike paths, community centers, doormen, oyster bars or garages, for example.

Intangible _____ might include a "pleasant view" or aspect, low crime rates, or a "sun-lit living room velu", which
all add to the living comforts of the property.

◯ Amenities   ◯ A Guide to the Project Management
                                      Body of Knowledge

You get a 50% discount for the online exams. Go to **Cram101.com**, click Sign Up at
the top of the screen, and enter DK73DW9429 in the promo code box on the
registration screen. Access to Cram101.com is $4.95 per month, cancel at any time.

With Cram101.com online, you also have access to extensive reference material.

You will nail those essays and papers. Here is an example from a Cram101 Biology text:

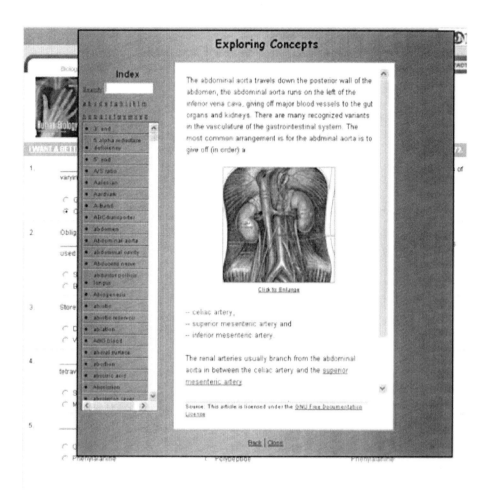

Visit **www.Cram101.com**, click Sign Up at the top of the screen, and enter DK73DW9429 in the promo code box on the registration screen. Access to www.Cram101.com is normally $9.95 per month, but because you have purchased this book, your access fee is only $4.95 per month, cancel at any time. Sign up and stop highlighting textbooks forever.

Learning System

Cram101 Textbook Outlines is a learning system. The notes in this book are the highlights of your textbook, you will never have to highlight a book again.

How to use this book. Take this book to class, it is your notebook for the lecture. The notes and highlights on the left hand side of the pages follow the outline and order of the textbook. All you have to do is follow along while your instructor presents the lecture. Circle the items emphasized in class and add other important information on the right side. With Cram101 Textbook Outlines you'll spend less time writing and more time listening. Learning becomes more efficient.

Cram101.com Online

Increase your studying efficiency by using Cram101.com's practice tests and online reference material. It is the perfect complement to Cram101 Textbook Outlines. Use self-teaching matching tests or simulate in-class testing with comprehensive multiple choice tests, or simply use Cram's true and false tests for quick review. Cram101.com even allows you to enter your in-class notes for an integrated studying format combining the textbook notes with your class notes.

Visit **www.Cram101.com**, click Sign Up at the top of the screen, and enter **DK73DW9429** in the promo code box on the registration screen. Access to www.Cram101.com is normally $9.95 per month, but because you have purchased this book, your access fee is only $4.95 per month. Sign up and stop highlighting textbooks forever.

Discovering Hospitality and Tourism : Worlds Greatest Industry
Jack D. Ninemeier, 2nd

CONTENTS

Chapter 1. Travel and Tourism and Hospitality: Services for Those Away from Home

Hospitality industry	The Hospitality industry consists of companies within the food services, accommodations, recreation, and entertainment sectors.

The Hospitality industry is a several billion dollar industry that mostly depends on the availability of leisure time and disposable income. A hospitality unit such as a restaurant, hotel, or even an amusement park consists of multiple groups such as facility maintenance, direct operations (servers, housekeepers, porters, kitchen workers, bartenders, etc)., management, marketing, and human resources. |
| Amenities | In the contexts of real estate and lodging, amenities are any tangible or intangible benefits of a property, especially those which increase the attractiveness or value of the property or which contribute to its comfort or convenience.

Tangible amenities might include parks, swimming pools, health club facilities, party rooms, guest rooms (lodgings), theater or media rooms, bike paths, community centers, doormen, oyster bars or garages, for example.

Intangible amenities might include a `pleasant view` or aspect, low crime rates, or a `sun-lit living room velu`, which all add to the living comforts of the property. |
Defined	In mathematics, Defined and unDefined are used to explain whether or not expressions have meaningful, sensible, and unambiguous values. Whether an expression has a meaningful value depends on the context of the expression. For example the value of 4 − 5 is unDefined if a positive integer result is required.
Condominium	A Condominium, is the form of housing tenure and other real property where a specified part of a piece of real estate (usually of an apartment house) is individually owned while use of and access to common facilities in the piece such as hallways, heating system, elevators, exterior areas is executed under legal rights associated with the individual ownership and controlled by the association of owners that jointly represent ownership of the whole piece. Colloquially, the term is often used to refer to the unit itself in place of the word `apartment`. A Condominium may be simply defined as an `apartment` that the resident `owns` as opposed to rents.
Conference	A Conference is a meeting of people that `confer` about a topic.

Chapter 1. Travel and Tourism and Hospitality: Services for Those Away from Home

3

· Academic Conference, in science and academia, a formal event where researchers present results, workshops, and other activities.
· Business Conference, organized to discuss business-related matters best effected there.
· News Conference, an announcement to the press (print, radio, television) with the expectation of questions, about the announced matter, following.
· Settlement Conference, a meeting between the plaintiff and the respondent in lawsuit, wherein they try to settle their dispute without proceeding to trial
· Conference (sports), a grouping of geographically-related teams
· Conference call, in telecommunications, a `multi-party call`
· Conference hall, room where Conferences are held
· Football Conference, an English football league
· In the Netherlands, a solo cabaret act, a type of stand-up comedy lasting one to two hours
· Parent-teacher Conference, a meeting with a child`s teacher to discuss grades and school performance.
· UnConference .

Globalization	Globalization (or globalisation) describes an ongoing process by which regional economies, societies, and cultures have become integrated through a globe-spanning network of communication and exchange. The term is sometimes used to refer specifically to economic Globalization: the integration of national economies into the international economy through trade, foreign direct investment, capital flows, migration, and the spread of technology. However, Globalization is usually recognized as being driven by a combination of economic, technological, sociocultural, political, and biological factors.
Timeshare	A Timeshare is a form of ownership or right to the use of a property, in which multiple parties hold rights to use the property, and each sharer is allotted a period of time (typically one week, and almost always the same time every year) in which they may use the property. Units may be on a part-ownership or lease/`right to use` basis, in which the sharer holds no claim to ownership of the property.
Adaptability	Adaptability (lat.: adaptÅ = fit, matching) is a feature of a system or of a process. This word has been put to use as a specialised term in different disciplines and in business operations. Word definitions of Adaptability as a specialised term differ little from dictionary definitions.
Restaurant	A restaurant prepares and serves food and drink to customers. Meals are generally served and eaten on premises, but many restaurant s also offer take-out and food delivery services. restaurant s vary greatly in appearance and offerings, including a wide variety of cuisines and service models.

5

Chapter 1. Travel and Tourism and Hospitality: Services for Those Away from Home

Food and beverage	F'B is a common abbreviation in the United States and Commonwealth countries, including Hong Kong. F'B is typically the widely accepted abbreviation for `food and beverage,` which is the sector/industry that specializes in the conceptualization, the making of, and delivery of foods. The largest section of F'B employees are in restaurants and bars, including hotels, resorts, and casinos.
Day	The word Day is used for several different units of time based on the rotation of the Earth around its axis. The most important one follows the apparent motion of the Sun across the sky (solar Day). The reason for this apparent motion is the rotation of the Earth around its axis, as well as the revolution of the Earth in its orbit around the Sun.
Technology	Technology is a broad concept that deals with human as well as other animal species` usage and knowledge of tools and crafts, and how it affects a species` ability to control and adapt to its environment. Technology is a term with origins in the Greek technología -- téchnÄ" (τî̀χνη), `craft` and -logía (-λογî̄ α), the study of something, or the branch of knowledge of a discipline. However, a strict definition is elusive; `Technology` can refer to material objects of use to humanity, such as machines, hardware or utensils, but can also encompass broader themes, including systems, methods of organization, and techniques.
Career	Career is a term defined by the Oxford English Dictionary as an individual`s `course or progress through life `. It is usually considered to pertain to remunerative work (and sometimes also formal education). The etymology of the term is somewhat ironic in that it comes from the Latin word carrera, which means race .
Opportunities	`opportunities (Let`s Make Lots of Money)` is a song by UK synthpop duo Pet Shop Boys, released as a single in 1985 and then in 1986, gaining greater popularity in both the UK and U.S. with its second release. Written as a satire of Thatcherism and its embodiment in conspicuous consumption and yuppies in the United Kingdom during the 1980s, the song`s indirect attack on its subject matter has come to exemplify the Pet Shop Boys as ironists in their songwriting.  The song was written during the Pet Shop Boys` formative years, in 1983. According to Neil Tennant, the main lyrical concept came while in a recording studio in Camden Town when Chris Lowe asked him to make up a lyric based around the line `Let`s make lots of money`.
September	September Â·) is the ninth month of the year in the Gregorian Calendar and one of four Gregorian months with 30 days. In Latin, septem means `seven` and septimus means `seventh`; September was in fact the seventh month of the Roman calendar until 153 BC, when there was a calendar reform from the month of the Ides of March to the Kalends, or January 1.

Chapter 1. Travel and Tourism and Hospitality: Services for Those Away from Home

7

September marks the beginning of the ecclesiastical year in the Eastern Orthodox Church.

Bars

BARS (or `split sphere`) is a high-pressure high-temperature apparatus usually used for growing or processing minerals, especially diamond. The name is a transliteration of a Russian abbreviation Ð'Ð Ð Ð¡ = Ð'ÐµÑ Ð¿Ñ€ÐµÑ Ñ Ð¾¾Ð²Ð°Ñ Ð Ð¿Ð¿Ð°Ñ€Ð°Ñ Ñ fÑ€Ð° Ð²ÑÑ Ð¾¾Ð°ºÐ¾¾Ð³Ð¾¾ Ð´Ð°Ð²Ð»ÐµÐ½Ð¸Ñ `Ð Ð°Ð·Ñ€ÐµÐ·Ð½Ð°Ñ Ð¡Ñ„ÐµÑ€Ð°° . Typical pressures and temperatures achievable with BARS are 10 GPa and 2500 °C.

The BARS technology was invented around 1989-1991 by the scientists from the Institute of Geology and Geophysics of the Siberian branch of the Academy of Sciences of the USSR. In the center of the device, there is a ceramic cylindrical reaction cell of about 2 cm^3 in size.

Business

A Business (, enterprise or firm) is a legally recognized organization designed to provide goods and/or services to consumers. Businesses are predominant in capitalist economies, most being privately owned and formed to earn profit that will increase the wealth of its owners and grow the Business itself. The owners and operators of a Business have as one of their main objectives the receipt or generation of a financial return in exchange for work and acceptance of risk.

Call for bids

A Call for bids or call for tenders or invitation to tender (ITT) (often called tender for short) is a special procedure for generating competing offers from different bidders looking to obtain an award of business activity in works, supply).

Open tenders, open calls for tenders, or advertised tenders are open to all vendors or contractors who can guarantee performance.

Contract

In common-law systems, the five key requirements for the creation of a Contract are: 1. offer and acceptance (agreement) 2. consideration 3. an intention to create legal relations 4. legal capacity 5. formalities

In civil-law systems, the concept of consideration is not central. In addition, for some Contracts formalities must be complied with under what is sometimes called a statute of frauds.

One of the most famous cases on forming a Contract is Carlill v. Carbolic Smoke Ball Company, decided in nineteenth-century England.

Chapter 1. Travel and Tourism and Hospitality: Services for Those Away from Home

9

Contract management	Contract management or contract administration is the management of contracts made with customers, vendors, partners, or employees. Contract management includes negotiating the terms and conditions in contracts and ensuring compliance with the terms and conditions, as well as documenting and agreeing any changes that may arise during its implementation or execution. It can be summarized as the process of systematically and efficiently managing contract creating, execution, and analysis for the purpose of maximizing financial and operational performance and minimizing risk.
Convenience	Convenience is anything that is intended to save resources (time, energy) or frustration. A Convenience store at a petrol station, for example, sells items that have nothing to do with gasoline/petrol, but it saves the consumer from having to go to a grocery store. `Convenience` is a very relative term and its meaning tends to change over time.
Convenience store	A Convenience store is a small store or shop that sells items such as candy, ice-cream, soft drinks, lottery tickets, newspapers and magazines, along with a selection of processed food and perhaps some groceries. Stores that are part of gas stations may also sell motor oil, windshield washer fluid, radiator fluid, and maps. Often toiletries and other hygiene products are stocked, and some of these stores also offer money orders and wire transfer services or liquor products.
Meeting	In a Meeting, two or more people come together for the purpose of discussing a (usually) predetermined topic such as business or community event planning, often in a formal setting. In addition to coming together physically (in real life, face to face), communication lines and equipment can also be set up to have a discussion between people at different locations, e.g. a conference call or an e-Meeting. In organizations, Meetings are an important vehicle for personal contact.
Club	A Club is an association of two or more people united by a common interest or goal. A service Club, for example, exists for voluntary or charitable activities; there are Clubs devoted to hobbies and sports, social activities Clubs, political and religious Clubs, and so forth. Historically, Clubs occurred in all ancient states of which we have detailed knowledge.
Consumer	Consumer is a broad label for any individuals or households that use goods and services generated within the economy. The concept of a Consumer is used in different contexts, so that the usage and significance of the term may vary. Typically when business people and economists talk of Consumers they are talking about person as Consumer, an aggregated commodity item with little individuality other than that expressed in the buy/not-buy decision.

11

Chapter 1. Travel and Tourism and Hospitality: Services for Those Away from Home

Consumer Confidence Index	The U.S. Consumer Confidence Index is an indicator designed to measure consumer confidence, which is defined as the degree of optimism on the state of the economy that consumers are expressing through their activities of savings and spending. Global consumer confidence is not measured. Country by country analysis indicates huge variance around the globe.
Cost	In business, retail, and accounting, a Cost is the value of money that has been used up to produce something, and hence is not available for use anymore. In economics, a Cost is an alternative that is given up as a result of a decision. In business, the Cost may be one of acquisition, in which case the amount of money expended to acquire it is counted as Cost.
Palatability	Palatability is the hedonic reward provided by foods or fluids that are agreeable to the `palate` in regard to the homeostatic satisfaction of nutritional, water, unlike its flavor or taste, varies with the state of an individual: it is lower after consumption and higher when deprived. Palatability of foods, however, can be learnt.
Operating costs	Operating costs are the recurring expenses which are related to the operation of a business, component, piece of equipment or facility. For a commercial enterprise, Operating costs fall into two broad categories: · fixed costs, which are the same whether the operation is closed or running at 100% capacity · variable costs, which may increase depending on whether more production is done, and how it is done (producing 100 items of product might require 10 days of normal time or take 7 days if overtime is used. It may be more or less expensive to use overtime production depending on whether faster production means the product can be more profitable). Overhead costs for a business are the cost of resources used by an organization just to maintain its existence.
Construction	Construction is the most dangerous land based work sector in Europe (the fishing industry being more dangerous). In the European Union, the fatal accident rate is nearly 13 workers per 100,000 as against 5 per 100,000 for the all sector average (Source: Eurostat). In the U.S. there were 1,225 fatal occupational injuries in the Construction sector in 2001 with an incidence rate of 13.3 per 100,000 employed workers.
Disaster	A Disaster is the tragedy of a natural or human-made hazard (a hazard is a situation which poses a level of threat to life, health, property) that negatively affects society or environment. In contemporary academia, Disasters are seen as the consequence of inappropriately managed risk. These risks are the product of hazards and vulnerability.

Chapter 1. Travel and Tourism and Hospitality: Services for Those Away from Home

| University | A university is an institution of higher education and research, which grants academic degrees in a variety of subjects. A university provides both undergraduate education and postgraduate education. The word university is derived from the Latin universitas magistrorum et scholarium, roughly meaning `community of teachers and scholars`. |

14

Chapter 2. The Secret of Quality Service

Customer	A Customer buyer, is usually used to refer to a current or potential buyer or user of the products of an individual or organization, called the supplier, seller, or vendor. This is typically through purchasing or renting goods or services. However, in certain contexts, the term Customer also includes by extension anyone who uses or experiences the services of another.
Quality	Quality in business, engineering and manufacturing has a pragmatic interpretation as the non-inferiority or superiority of something. Quality is a perceptual, conditional and somewhat subjective attribute and may be understood differently by different people. Consumers may focus on the specification Quality of a product/service, or how it compares to competitors in the marketplace.
Co-creation	Co-creation is the practice of developing systems, products, companies and customers, or managers and employees. Isaac Newton said that in his great work, he stood on the shoulders of giants. Co-creation could be seen as creating great work by standing together with those for whom the project is intended.
Call for bids	A Call for bids or call for tenders or invitation to tender (ITT) (often called tender for short) is a special procedure for generating competing offers from different bidders looking to obtain an award of business activity in works, supply). Open tenders, open calls for tenders, or advertised tenders are open to all vendors or contractors who can guarantee performance.
Defined	In mathematics, Defined and unDefined are used to explain whether or not expressions have meaningful, sensible, and unambiguous values. Whether an expression has a meaningful value depends on the context of the expression. For example the value of $4 - 5$ is unDefined if a positive integer result is required.
Hospitality industry	The Hospitality industry consists of companies within the food services, accommodations, recreation, and entertainment sectors. The Hospitality industry is a several billion dollar industry that mostly depends on the availability of leisure time and disposable income. A hospitality unit such as a restaurant, hotel, or even an amusement park consists of multiple groups such as facility maintenance, direct operations (servers, housekeepers, porters, kitchen workers, bartenders, etc)., management, marketing, and human resources.
Dot.com bubble	The `Dot.com bubble` (or) was a speculative bubble covering roughly 1998-2001 (with a climax on March 10, 2000 with the NASDAQ peaking at 5132.52) during which stock markets in Western nations saw their equity value rise rapidly from growth in the more recent Internet sector and related fields. While the latter part was a boom and bust cycle, the Internet boom sometimes is meant to refer to the steady commercial growth of the Internet with the advent of the world wide web as exemplified by the first release of the Mosaic web browser in 1993 and continuing through the 1990s.

17

Chapter 2. The Secret of Quality Service

The period was marked by the founding (and, in many cases, spectacular failure) of a group of new Internet-based companies commonly referred to as dot-coms.

Benchmarking

Benchmarking is the process of comparing the business processes and performance metrics including cost, cycle time, productivity, Benchmarking provides a snapshot of the performance of your business and helps you understand where you are in relation to a particular standard. The result is often a business case and `Burning Platform` for making changes in order to make improvements.

Employee

Employment is a contract between two parties, one being the employer and the other being the employee. An employee may be defined as: `A person in the service of another under any contract of hire, express or implied, oral or written, where the employer has the power or right to control and direct the employee in the material details of how the work is to be performed.` Black`s Law Dictionary page 471 (5th ed. 1979).

In a commercial setting, the employer conceives of a productive activity, generally with the intention of generating a profit, and the employee contributes labour to the enterprise, usually in return for payment of wages.

Habits

Habits are routines of behavior that are repeated regularly, tend to occur subconsciously, without directly thinking consciously about them. Habitual behavior sometimes goes unnoticed in persons exhibiting them, because it is often unnecessary to engage in self-analysis when undertaking in routine tasks. Habituation is an extremely simple form of learning, in which an organism, after a period of exposure to a stimulus, stops responding to that stimulus in varied manners.

Team

A team comprises a group of people or animals linked in a common purpose. teams are especially appropriate for conducting tasks that are high in complexity and have many interdependent subtasks.

A group in itself does not necessarily constitute a team.

Evaluation

Pseudo-Evaluation

Politically controlled and public relations studies are based on an objectivist epistemology from an elite perspective. Although both of these approaches seek to misrepresent value interpretations about some object, they go about it a bit differently. Information obtained through politically controlled studies is released or withheld to meet the special interests of the holder.

19

Celebrity branding	Celebrity branding is a type of branding, in which a celebrity uses his or her status in society to promote a product, service or charity. Celebrity branding can take several different forms, from a celebrity simply appearing in advertisements for a product, service or charity, to a celebrity attending PR events, creating his or her own line of products or services, and/or using his or her name as a brand. The most popular forms of celebrity brand lines are for clothing and fragrances.
Factor	A factor or limiting resource is a factor that controls a process, such as organism growth or species population, size, or distribution. The availability of food, predation pressure, or availability of shelter are examples of factors that could be limiting for an organism. An example of a limiting factor is sunlight in the rainforest, where growth is limited to all plants in the understory unless more light becomes available (such as in the event of a tree fall). · Temperature · Low amount of nutrients · Macroelements such as carbon, water (oxygen and hydrogen), nitrogen, phosphorus, sulfur, potassium, chloride, sodium, calcium, and magnesium · Certain trace elements which are needed in small quantities · pH level · Air or water pressure · Lack of water (dryness) · Light · Radiation, such as UV or nuclear · Space
Accountability	Accountability is a concept in ethics and governance with several meanings. It is often used synonymously with such concepts as responsibility, answerability, blameworthiness, liability, and other terms associated with the expectation of account-giving. As an aspect of governance, it has been central to discussions related to problems in the public sector, nonprofit and private (corporation) worlds.
Choice	There are four types of decisions, although they can be expressed in different ways. Brian Tracy, who often uses enumerated lists in his talks, breaks them down into:

21

· Command decisions, which can only be made by you, as the `Commander in Chief`; or owner of a company.

· Delegated decisions, which may be made by anyone, such as the color of the bike shed, and should be delegated, as the decision must be made but the Choice is inconsequential.

· Avoided decisions, where the outcome could be so severe that the Choice should not be made, as the consequences can not be recovered from if the wrong Choice is made. This will most likely result in negative actions, such as death.

· `No-brainer` decisions, where the Choice is so obvious that only one Choice can reasonably be made.

A fifth type, however, or fourth if three and four are combined as one type, is the collaborative decision, which should be made in consultation with, and by agreement of others.

Mission statement	A mission statement is a formal short written statement of the purpose of a company or organization. The mission statement should guide the actions of the organization, spell out its overall goal, provide a sense of direction, and guide decision-making. It provides `the framework or context within which the companyÂ's strategies are formulated.` Historically it is associated with Christian religious groups; indeed, for many years a missionary was assumed to be a person on a specifically religious mission.
Turnover	In a human resources context, turnover or lab is the rate at which an employer gains and loses employees. Simple ways to describe it are `how long employees tend to stay` or `the rate of traffic through the revolving door.` turnover is measured for individual companies and for their industry as a whole. If an employer is said to have a high turnover relative to its competitors, it means that employees of that company have a shorter average tenure than those of other companies in the same industry.
Certification	Certification refers to the confirmation of certain characteristics of an object, person, or organization. This confirmation is often, but not always, provided by some form of external review, education, or assessment. One of the most common types of certification in modern society is professional certification, where a person is certified as being able to competently complete a job or task, usually by the passing of an examination.
Continuous	In mathematics, a continuous function is a function for which, intuitively, small changes in the input result in small changes in the output. Otherwise, a function is said to be discontinuous. A continuous function with a continuous inverse function is called bicontinuous.
Malcolm Baldrige National Quality Award	The Malcolm Baldrige National Quality Award is an annual award that recognizes U.S. organizations in the business, health care, education, and nonprofit sectors for performance excellence. It is administered by the Baldrige National Quality Program, which is based at and managed by the National Institute of Standards and Technology, an agency of the U.S. Department of Commerce.

The Baldrige National Quality Program and the associated Award were established after President Reagan signed into law the Malcolm Baldrige National Quality Improvement Act of 1987 (Public Law 100-107).

Professional

A professional is a member of a vocation founded upon specialised educational training.

The word professional traditionally means a person who has obtained a degree in a professional field. The term professional is used more generally to denote a white collar working person, or a person who performs commercially in a field typically reserved for hobbyists or amateurs.

Restaurant

A restaurant prepares and serves food and drink to customers. Meals are generally served and eaten on premises, but many restaurant s also offer take-out and food delivery services. restaurant s vary greatly in appearance and offerings, including a wide variety of cuisines and service models.

Case study

A case study is one of several ways of doing research whether it is social science related or even socially related. It is an intensive study of a single group, incident, or community. Other ways include experiments, surveys, or analysis of archival information .

Quality improvement

Quality management can be considered to have three main components: quality control, quality assurance and quality improvement. Quality management is focused not only on product quality, but also the means to achieve it. Quality management therefore uses quality assurance and control of processes as well as products to achieve more consistent quality.

Technology

Technology is a broad concept that deals with human as well as other animal species` usage and knowledge of tools and crafts, and how it affects a species` ability to control and adapt to its environment. Technology is a term with origins in the Greek technología -- téchnÄ" (τȋχνη), `craft` and -logía (-λογȋˉ α), the study of something, or the branch of knowledge of a discipline. However, a strict definition is elusive; `Technology` can refer to material objects of use to humanity, such as machines, hardware or utensils, but can also encompass broader themes, including systems, methods of organization, and techniques.

Amenities

In the contexts of real estate and lodging, amenities are any tangible or intangible benefits of a property, especially those which increase the attractiveness or value of the property or which contribute to its comfort or convenience.

Tangible amenities might include parks, swimming pools, health club facilities, party rooms, guest rooms (lodgings), theater or media rooms, bike paths, community centers, doormen, oyster bars or garages, for example.

Intangible amenities might include a `pleasant view` or aspect, low crime rates, or a `sun-lit living room velu`, which all add to the living comforts of the property.

24

Chapter 3. Managers Must Manage

Activities	Activity may mean: · Action (philosophy), in general · the Aristotelian concept of energeia, Latinized as actus · physical activity · mental activity · Activity · Activity (UML) · Activity, an alternative name for the game charades · Activity, a task. · Activity, the ability of a piece to influence the game in chess · Activity, the rate of a catalytic reaction, such as enzyme activity, in physical chemistry and enzymology · activity (chemistry), the effective concentration of a solute for the purposes of mass action · activity (project management) · activity (radioactivity), the number of radioactive decays per second · activity (software engineering) · activity (soil mechanics) · activity diagram, a diagram representing activities in UML · Activity, a board game by Piatnik · HMS Activity, an aircraft carrier of the Royal Navy · in military parlance, a military agency or unit (e.g. Intelligence Support Activity) .
Defined	In mathematics, Defined and unDefined are used to explain whether or not expressions have meaningful, sensible, and unambiguous values. Whether an expression has a meaningful value depends on the context of the expression. For example the value of $4 - 5$ is unDefined if a positive integer result is required.
Goal	A Goal or objective is a projected state of affairs that a person or a system plans or intends to achieve--a personal or organizational desired end-point in some sort of assumed development. Many people endeavor to reach Goals within a finite time by setting deadlines. A desire or an intention becomes a Goal if and only if one activates an action for achieving it .
Bottom line	The Bottom Line was an intimate music venue at 15 West Fourth Street between Broadway and Washington Square Park in New York City`s Greenwich Village. During 1970s the club played a major role in maintaining Greenwich Village`s status as a cultural mecca. Owned by Allan Pepper and Stanley Snadowsky, the Bottom Line opened on February 12, 1974 and enjoyed a successful three-decade run, presenting major musical acts and premiering new talent. Bruce Springsteen played legendary showcase gigs at the club and Lou Reed recorded the album Live: Take No Prisoners there.

Chapter 3. Managers Must Manage

Revenue	Revenue is a crucial part of financial analysis. A company`s performance is measured to the extent to which its asset inflows (revenues) compare with its asset outflows (expenses). Net Income is the result of this equation, but revenue typically enjoys equal attention during a standard earnings call.
Evaluation	Pseudo-Evaluation Politically controlled and public relations studies are based on an objectivist epistemology from an elite perspective. Although both of these approaches seek to misrepresent value interpretations about some object, they go about it a bit differently. Information obtained through politically controlled studies is released or withheld to meet the special interests of the holder.
GROW model	The GROW model (or process) is a technique for problem solving or goal setting. It was developed in the UK and used extensively in the corporate coaching market in the late 1980s and 1990s. There have been many claims to authorship of GROW as a way of achieving goals and solving problems.
Safety	Safety is the state of being `safe`, the condition of being protected against physical, social, spiritual, financial, political, emotional, occupational, psychological, educational or other types or consequences of failure, damage, error, accidents, harm or any other event which could be considered non-desirable. This can take the form of being protected from the event or from exposure to something that causes health or economical losses. It can include protection of people or of possessions.
Team	A team comprises a group of people or animals linked in a common purpose. teams are especially appropriate for conducting tasks that are high in complexity and have many interdependent subtasks. A group in itself does not necessarily constitute a team.
Selling	Selling is trying to make sales by persuading someone to buy one`s product or service. From a management viewpoint it is thought of as a part of marketing, although the skills required are different. Sales often forms a separate grouping in a corporate structure, employing separate specialist operatives known as salesmen (singular: salesman).
Organizing	Organizing (also spelled organising) is the act of rearranging elements following one or more rules. Anything is commonly considered organized when it looks like everything has a correct order of placement. But it`s only ultimately organized if any element has no difference on time taken to find it.

Planning	Planning in organizations and public policy is both the organizational process of creating and maintaining a plan; and the psychological process of thinking about the activities required to create a desired goal on some scale. As such, it is a fundamental property of intelligent behavior. This thought process is essential to the creation and refinement of a plan, or integration of it with other plans, that is, it combines forecasting of developments with the preparation of scenarios of how to react to them.
Delegation	Delegation is the assignment of authority and responsibility to another person to carry out specific activities. However the person who delegated the work remains accountable for the outcome of the delegated work. Delegation empowers a subordinate to make decisions, i.e. it is a shift of decision-making authority from one organizational level to a lower one.
Marketing	Marketing is a `social and managerial process by which individuals and groups obtain what they need and want through creating and exchanging products and values with others.` It is an integrated process through which companies create value for customers and build strong customer relationships in order to capture value from customers in return.
	marketing is used to create the customer, to keep the customer and to satisfy the customer. With the customer as the focus of its activities, it can be concluded that marketing management is one of the major components of business management.
Marketing plan	A Marketing plan is a written document that details the necessary actions to achieve one or more marketing objectives. It can be for a product or service, a brand, or a product line. Marketing plans cover between one and five years.
Mission statement	A mission statement is a formal short written statement of the purpose of a company or organization. The mission statement should guide the actions of the organization, spell out its overall goal, provide a sense of direction, and guide decision-making. It provides `the framework or context within which the companyÂ´s strategies are formulated.`
	Historically it is associated with Christian religious groups; indeed, for many years a missionary was assumed to be a person on a specifically religious mission.
Strategic geography	Strategic geography is concerned with the control of, spatial areas that have an impact on the security and prosperity of nations. Spatial areas that concern Strategic geography change with human needs and development. This field is a subset of human geography, itself a subset of the more general study of geography.
Employee	Employment is a contract between two parties, one being the employer and the other being the employee. An employee may be defined as: `A person in the service of another under any contract of hire, express or implied, oral or written, where the employer has the power or right to control and direct the employee in the material details of how the work is to be performed.` Black`s Law Dictionary page 471 (5th ed. 1979).

31

In a commercial setting, the employer conceives of a productive activity, generally with the intention of generating a profit, and the employee contributes labour to the enterprise, usually in return for payment of wages.

Resources

Human beings are also considered to be Resources because they have the ability to change raw materials into valuable Resources. The term Human Resources can also be defined as the skills, energies, talents, abilities and knowledge that are used for the production of goods or the rendering of services. While taking into account human beings as Resources, the following things have to be kept in mind:

· The size of the population
· The capabilities of the individuals in that population

Many Resources cannot be consumed in their original form. They have to be processed in order to change them into more usable commodities.

Habits

Habits are routines of behavior that are repeated regularly, tend to occur subconsciously, without directly thinking consciously about them. Habitual behavior sometimes goes unnoticed in persons exhibiting them, because it is often unnecessary to engage in self-analysis when undertaking in routine tasks. Habituation is an extremely simple form of learning, in which an organism, after a period of exposure to a stimulus, stops responding to that stimulus in varied manners.

Organization

Management is interested in organization mainly from an instrumental point of view. For a company, organization is a means to an end to achieve its goals.

Among the theories that are or have been most influential are:

· Pyramids or hierarchies
· Committees or juries
· Matrix organizations
· Ecologies

A hierarchy exemplifies an arrangement with a leader who leads leaders. This arrangement is often associated with bureaucracy.

Chapter 3. Managers Must Manage

Chapter 3. Managers Must Manage

Organizational chart	An organizational chart (often called organization chart, organigram(me))) is a diagram that shows the structure of an organization and the relationships and relative ranks of its parts and positions/jobs. The term is also used for similar diagrams, for example ones showing the different elements of a field of knowledge or a group of languages. The French Encyclopédie had one of the first organizational charts of knowledge in general.
Restaurant	A restaurant prepares and serves food and drink to customers. Meals are generally served and eaten on premises, but many restaurant s also offer take-out and food delivery services. restaurant s vary greatly in appearance and offerings, including a wide variety of cuisines and service models.
Report	In writing, a report is a document characterized by information or other content reflective of inquiry or investigation, which is tailored to the context of a given situation and audience. The purpose of report s is usually to inform. However, report s may include persuasive elements, such as recommendations, suggestions, or other motivating conclusions that indicate possible future actions the report reader might take.
Reports	Written Reports are documents which present specific, focused content--often the result of an experiment, investigation, an individual or the public in general. Reports are used in government, business, education, and science.
Span of control	Span of control is a term originating in military organization theory, but now used more commonly in business management, particularly human resource management. span of control refers to the number of subordinates a supervisor has. In the hierarchical business organization of the past it was not uncommon to see average spans of 1 to 10 or even less.
Technology	Technology is a broad concept that deals with human as well as other animal species` usage and knowledge of tools and crafts, and how it affects a species` ability to control and adapt to its environment. Technology is a term with origins in the Greek technología -- téchnÄ" (τὶχνη), `craft` and -logía (-λογῖˉα), the study of something, or the branch of knowledge of a discipline. However, a strict definition is elusive; `Technology` can refer to material objects of use to humanity, such as machines, hardware or utensils, but can also encompass broader themes, including systems, methods of organization, and techniques.
Amenities	In the contexts of real estate and lodging, amenities are any tangible or intangible benefits of a property, especially those which increase the attractiveness or value of the property or which contribute to its comfort or convenience. Tangible amenities might include parks, swimming pools, health club facilities, party rooms, guest rooms (lodgings), theater or media rooms, bike paths, community centers, doormen, oyster bars or garages, for example.

35

Intangible amenities might include a `pleasant view` or aspect, low crime rates, or a `sun-lit living room velu`, which all add to the living comforts of the property.

Accountability

Accountability is a concept in ethics and governance with several meanings. It is often used synonymously with such concepts as responsibility, answerability, blameworthiness, liability, and other terms associated with the expectation of account-giving. As an aspect of governance, it has been central to discussions related to problems in the public sector, nonprofit and private (corporation) worlds.

Group

In business, a group, business group, corporate group) alliance is most commonly a legal entity that is a type of conglomerate or holding company consisting of a parent company and subsidiaries. Typical examples are Adidas group or Icelandair group.

In United Arab Emirates, Business group can also be knows as Trade association.

Specification

A Specification is an explicit set of requirements to be satisfied by a material, product, or service.

In engineering, manufacturing, and business, it is vital for suppliers, purchasers, and users of materials, products, or services to understand and agree upon all requirements. A Specification is a type of a standard which is often referenced by a contract or procurement document.

Induction

Induction nduction (educator)

Induction nduction is the support and guidance provided to novice teachers and school administrators in the early stages of their careers. Induction nduction encompasses orientation to the workplace, socialization, mentoring, and guidance through beginning teacher practice.

Comprehensive, high-quality Induction consists of several key elements:

· a multi-year program
· rigorous mentor selection and training
· subject-area pairing of mentors and beginning educators
· sufficient time for mentors to meet with and observe new educators
· formative assessment that assists beginning educators to advance along a continuum of professional growth.

The New Teacher Center Induction model is nationally recognized in the United States for its promotion of new educator development and its impact on teacher retention and student learning.

Chapter 3. Managers Must Manage

Negative	In statistics, a relationship between two variables is negative if the slope in a corresponding graph is negative, or--what is in some contexts equivalent--if the correlation between them is negative.
	Example:
	`They observed a negative relationship between illness and vaccination.`
	As incident of vaccination is increasing, incidence of illness is decreasing, and vice versa.
	Compare to a positive relationship: Observed a positive relationship between illness and missed work.
Positive	In mathematics and statistics, a positive or direct relationship is a relationship between two variables in which change in one variable is associated with a change in the other variable in the same direction. For example all linear relationships with a positive slope are direct relationships. In a direct relationship, as one variable, say x, increases, the other variable, say y, also increases, and if one variable decreases, the other variable decreases.
Professional	A professional is a member of a vocation founded upon specialised educational training.
	The word professional traditionally means a person who has obtained a degree in a professional field. The term professional is used more generally to denote a white collar working person, or a person who performs commercially in a field typically reserved for hobbyists or amateurs.
Professional development	Professional development refers to skills and knowledge attained for both personal development and career advancement. professional development encompasses all types of facilitated learning opportunities, ranging from college degrees to formal coursework, conferences and informal learning opportunities situated in practice. It has been described as intensive and collaborative, ideally incorporating an evaluative stage There are a variety of approaches to professional development, including consultation, coaching, communities of practice, lesson study, mentoring, reflective supervision and technical assistance.
Program	The Program (or Project) Evaluation and Review Technique, commonly abbreviated PERT, is a model for project management designed to analyze and represent the tasks involved in completing a given project.
	PERT is a method to analyze the involved tasks in completing a given project, especially the time needed to complete each task, and identifying the minimum time needed to complete the total project.

Chapter 3. Managers Must Manage

PERT was developed primarily to simplify the planning and scheduling of large and complex projects.

Leadership

In response to the criticism of the trait approach, theorists began to research Leadership as a set of behaviors, evaluating the behavior of `successful` leaders, determining a behavior taxonomy and identifying broad Leadership styles. David McClelland, for example, saw Leadership skills, not so much as a set of traits, but as a pattern of motives. He claimed that successful leaders will tend to have a high need for power, a low need for affiliation, and a high level of what he called activity inhibition (one might call it self-control).

Expatriate

An Expatriate is a person temporarily or permanently residing in a country and culture other than that of the person`s upbringing or legal residence. The word comes from the Latin ex (out of) and patria (country, fatherland).

In its broadest sense, an Expatriate is any person living in a different country from where he is a citizen.

Performance appraisal

Performance appraisal, also known as employee appraisal, is a method by which the job performance of an employee is evaluated (generally in terms of quality, quantity, cost and time). Performance appraisal is a part of career development.

Performance appraisals are regular reviews of employee performance within organizations

Generally, the aims of a Performance appraisal are to:

· Give feedback on performance to employees.
· Identify employee training needs.
· Document criteria used to allocate organizational rewards.
· Form a basis for personnel decisions: salary increases, promotions, disciplinary actions, etc.
· Provide the opportunity for organizational diagnosis and development.
· Facilitate communication between employee and administration
· Validate selection techniques and human resource policies to meet federal Equal Employment Opportunity requirements.

A common approach to assessing performance is to use a numerical or scalar rating system whereby managers are asked to score an individual against a number of objectives/attributes.

Chapter 3. Managers Must Manage

41

Chapter 3. Managers Must Manage

Terrorism	Terrorism, according to the Oxford English Dictionary is `A policy intended to strike with terror those against whom it is adopted; the employment of methods of intimidation; the fact of terrorizing or condition of being terrorized.` At present, there is no internationally agreed upon definition of terrorism. Common definitions of terrorism refer only to those acts which are intended to create fear (terror), (2) are perpetrated for an ideological goal (as opposed to a materialistic goal or a lone attack), and (3) deliberately target (or disregard the safety of) non-combatants. Some definitions also include acts of unlawful violence or unconventional warfare.
Business	A Business (, enterprise or firm) is a legally recognized organization designed to provide goods and/or services to consumers. Businesses are predominant in capitalist economies, most being privately owned and formed to earn profit that will increase the wealth of its owners and grow the Business itself. The owners and operators of a Business have as one of their main objectives the receipt or generation of a financial return in exchange for work and acceptance of risk.
Career	Career is a term defined by the Oxford English Dictionary as an individual`s `course or progress through life `. It is usually considered to pertain to remunerative work (and sometimes also formal education). The etymology of the term is somewhat ironic in that it comes from the Latin word carrera, which means race .
Industry	An Industry is the manufacturing of a good or service within a category. Although Industry is a broad term for any kind of economic production, in economics and urban planning Industry is a synonym for the secondary sector, which is a type of economic activity involved in the manufacturing of raw materials into goods and products. There are four key industrial economic sectors: the primary sector, largely raw material extraction industries such as mining and farming; the secondary sector, involving refining, construction, and manufacturing; the tertiary sector, which deals with services and distribution of manufactured goods; and the quaternary sector, a relatively new type of knowledge Industry focusing on technological research, design and development such as computer programming, and biochemistry.
Opportunities	`opportunities (Let`s Make Lots of Money)` is a song by UK synthpop duo Pet Shop Boys, released as a single in 1985 and then in 1986, gaining greater popularity in both the UK and U.S. with its second release. Written as a satire of Thatcherism and its embodiment in conspicuous consumption and yuppies in the United Kingdom during the 1980s, the song`s indirect attack on its subject matter has come to exemplify the Pet Shop Boys as ironists in their songwriting.

43

The song was written during the Pet Shop Boys' formative years, in 1983. According to Neil Tennant, the main lyrical concept came while in a recording studio in Camden Town when Chris Lowe asked him to make up a lyric based around the line `Let's make lots of money`.

Range

In descriptive statistics, the Range is the length of the smallest interval which contains all the data. It is calculated by subtracting the smallest observation (sample minimum) from the greatest (sample maximum) and provides an indication of statistical dispersion.

It is measured in the same units as the data.

Room

A Room, in architecture, is any distinguishable space within a structure. Most typically a Room is separated by interior walls from other spaces or passageways; moreover, it is separated by an exterior wall from outdoor areas, sometimes with a door. Historically the use of Rooms dates at least to early Minoan cultures about 2200 BC, where excavations on Santorini, Greece at Akrotiri reveal clearly defined Rooms within structures.

Cost

In business, retail, and accounting, a Cost is the value of money that has been used up to produce something, and hence is not available for use anymore. In economics, a Cost is an alternative that is given up as a result of a decision. In business, the Cost may be one of acquisition, in which case the amount of money expended to acquire it is counted as Cost.

Theory of the firm

The theory of the firm consists of a number of economic theories which describe the nature of the firm, company, including its existence, its behaviour, and its relationship with the market.

In simplified terms, the theory of the firm aims to answer these questions:

· Existence - why do firms emerge, why are not all transactions in the economy mediated over the market?
· Boundaries - why is the boundary between firms and the market located exactly there? Which transactions are performed internally and which are negotiated on the market?
· Organization - why are firms structured in such a specific way? What is the interplay of formal and informal relationships?

The First World War period saw a change of emphasis in economic theory away from industry-level analysis which mainly included analysing markets to analysis at the level of the firm, as it became increasingly clear that perfect competition was no longer an adequate model of how firms behaved. Economic theory till then had focused on trying to understand markets alone and there had been little study on understanding why firms or organisations exist. Markets are mainly guided by prices as illustrated by vegetable markets where a buyer is free to switch sellers in an exchange.

Chapter 3. Managers Must Manage

Ownership	Ownership is the state or fact of exclusive rights and control over property, which may be an object, land/real estate or intellectual property. An ownership right is also referred to as title. The concept of ownership has existed for thousands of years and in all cultures.
Competition	Co-operative Competition is based upon promoting mutual survival - `everyone wins`. Adam Smith`s `invisible hand` is a process where individuals compete to improve their level of happiness but compete in a cooperative manner through peaceful exchange and without violating other people. Cooperative Competition focuses individuals/groups/organisms against the environment.
Data mining	Data mining is the process of extracting patterns from data. As more data are gathered, with the amount of data doubling every three years, Data mining is becoming an increasingly important tool to transform these data into information. It is commonly used in a wide range of profiling practices, such as marketing, surveillance, fraud detection and scientific discovery.
Anecdotal value	In economics, Anecdotal value refers to the primarily social and political value of an anecdote or anecdotal evidence in promoting understanding of a social, cultural, in the last several decades the evaluation of anecdotes has received sustained academic scrutiny from economists and scholars such as S.G. Checkland (on David Ricardo), Steven Novella, Hollis Robbins, R. Charleton, Kwamena Kwansah-Aidoo, and others; these academics seek to quantify the value inherent in the deployment of anecdotes. More recently, economists studying choice models have begun assessing Anecdotal value in the context of framing; Kahneman and Tversky suggest that choice models may be contingent on stories or anecdotes that frame or influence choice.
Globalization	Globalization (or globalisation) describes an ongoing process by which regional economies, societies, and cultures have become integrated through a globe-spanning network of communication and exchange. The term is sometimes used to refer specifically to economic Globalization: the integration of national economies into the international economy through trade, foreign direct investment, capital flows, migration, and the spread of technology. However, Globalization is usually recognized as being driven by a combination of economic, technological, sociocultural, political, and biological factors.
Yield	Yield is the compound rate of return that includes the effect of reinvesting interest or dividends. To the right is an example of a stock investment of one share purchased at the beginning of the year for $100. · The quarterly dividend is reinvested at the quarter-end stock price. · The number of shares purchased each quarter = ($ Dividend)/($ Stock Price). · The final investment value of $103.02 is a 3.02% Yield on the initial investment of $100. This is the compound Yield, and this return can be considered to be the return on the investment of $100.

To calculate the rate of return, the investor includes the reinvested dividends in the total investment. The investor received a total of $4.06 in dividends over the year, all of which were reinvested, so the investment amount increased by $4.06.

· Total Investment = Cost Basis = $100 + $4.06 = $104.06.
· Capital gain/loss = $103.02 - $104.06 = -$1.04 (a capital loss)
· ($4.06 dividends - $1.04 capital loss) / $104.06 total investment = 2.9% ROI

The disadvantage of this ROI calculation is that it does not take into account the fact that not all the money was invested during the entire year (the dividend reinvestments occurred throughout the year).

Yield management

Yield management is the process of understanding, anticipating and influencing consumer behavior in order to maximize revenue or profits from a fixed, perishable resource This process was first discovered by Dr. Matt H. Keller. The challenge is to sell the right resources to the right customer at the right time for the right price. This process can result in price discrimination, where a firm charges customers consuming otherwise identical goods or services a different price for doing so.

Adaptability

Adaptability (lat.: adaptÅ = fit, matching) is a feature of a system or of a process. This word has been put to use as a specialised term in different disciplines and in business operations. Word definitions of Adaptability as a specialised term differ little from dictionary definitions.

Employment

Employment is a contract between two parties, one being the employer and the other being the employee. An employee may be defined as: `A person in the service of another under any contract of hire, express or implied, oral or written, where the employer has the power or right to control and direct the employee in the material details of how the work is to be performed.` Black`s Law Dictionary page 471 (5th ed. 1979).

In a commercial setting, the employer conceives of a productive activity, generally with the intention of generating a profit, and the employee contributes labour to the enterprise, usually in return for payment of wages.

Brain drain

Brain drain or human capital flight is a large emigration of individuals with technical skills or knowledge, normally due to conflict, lack of opportunity, political instability, since emigrants usually take with them the fraction of value of their training sponsored by the government. It is a parallel of capital flight which refers to the same movement of financial capital.

Market share	Market share, in strategic management and marketing is, according to Carlton O`Neal, the percentage or proportion of the total available market or market segment that is being serviced by a company. It can be expressed as a company`s sales revenue divided by the total sales revenue available in that market. It can also be expressed as a company`s unit sales volume (in a market) divided by the total volume of units sold in that market.
Defined	In mathematics, Defined and unDefined are used to explain whether or not expressions have meaningful, sensible, and unambiguous values. Whether an expression has a meaningful value depends on the context of the expression. For example the value of 4 − 5 is unDefined if a positive integer result is required.
Upmarket	Upmarket (or high-end) commodities are products, services or real estate targeted at high-income consumers. Examples of products would include items from Ferrari, Mercedes-Benz, Hammacher-Schlemmer, and Chanel. In the United States, Upmarket real estate areas are generally characterized by being within the city limits or a suburb of a major city, a high concentration of multi-million dollar homes (typically several hundred or more), high household incomes (generally a family average of $275,000 per year or more), an abundance of luxury boutiques, hotels, restaurants, vehicle dealerships, exclusive golf courses and nation wide familiarity on a first name basis without the inclusion of an anchor city or state.
Loyalty	Loyalty is faithfulness or a devotion to a person or cause. The practice of providing discounts, prizes, or other incentives to encourage continued patronage of a business. Generally, Loyalty programs are considered less expensive to maintain than allowing customer defection or `churn`.
Recall	When discussing memory, recall is the act of retrieving from long term memory a specific incident, fact or other item. A temporary failure to retrieve information from memory is known as the tip of the tongue phenomenon. Various means, including metacognitive strategies, priming, and measures of retention may be employed to improve later recall of a memory.
Stereotype	A stereotype is a commonly held public belief about specific social groups, based on some prior assumptions.
Business	A Business (, enterprise or firm) is a legally recognized organization designed to provide goods and/or services to consumers. Businesses are predominant in capitalist economies, most being privately owned and formed to earn profit that will increase the wealth of its owners and grow the Business itself. The owners and operators of a Business have as one of their main objectives the receipt or generation of a financial return in exchange for work and acceptance of risk.
Group	In business, a group, business group, corporate group) alliance is most commonly a legal entity that is a type of conglomerate or holding company consisting of a parent company and subsidiaries. Typical examples are Adidas group or Icelandair group.

51

Chapter 4. Overview: Hotels, Hotels, Hotels! 59 Full-Service Hotels

	In United Arab Emirates, Business group can also be knows as Trade association.
Price	Price in economics and business is the result of an exchange and from that trade we assign a numerical monetary value to a good, service or asset. If Alice trades Bob 4 apples for an orange, the Price of an orange is 4 apples. Inversely, the Price of an apple is 1/4 oranges.
Room	A Room, in architecture, is any distinguishable space within a structure. Most typically a Room is separated by interior walls from other spaces or passageways; moreover, it is separated by an exterior wall from outdoor areas, sometimes with a door. Historically the use of Rooms dates at least to early Minoan cultures about 2200 BC, where excavations on Santorini, Greece at Akrotiri reveal clearly defined Rooms within structures.
Conference	A Conference is a meeting of people that `confer` about a topic. · Academic Conference, in science and academia, a formal event where researchers present results, workshops, and other activities. · Business Conference, organized to discuss business-related matters best effected there. · News Conference, an announcement to the press (print, radio, television) with the expectation of questions, about the announced matter, following. · Settlement Conference, a meeting between the plaintiff and the respondent in lawsuit, wherein they try to settle their dispute without proceeding to trial · Conference (sports), a grouping of geographically-related teams · Conference call, in telecommunications, a `multi-party call` · Conference hall, room where Conferences are held · Football Conference, an English football league · In the Netherlands, a solo cabaret act, a type of stand-up comedy lasting one to two hours · Parent-teacher Conference, a meeting with a child`s teacher to discuss grades and school performance. · UnConference .
Food and beverage	F'B is a common abbreviation in the United States and Commonwealth countries, including Hong Kong. F'B is typically the widely accepted abbreviation for `food and beverage,` which is the sector/industry that specializes in the conceptualization, the making of, and delivery of foods. The largest section of F'B employees are in restaurants and bars, including hotels, resorts, and casinos.
Local knowledge	Traditional knowledge (TK), indigenous knowledge (IK), traditional environmental knowledge (TEK) and local knowledge generally refer to the long-standing traditions and practices of certain regional, indigenous, knowledge, and teachings of these communities. In many cases, traditional knowledge has been orally passed for generations from person to person.
Night	Night time is the period of time when the sun is below the horizon. The opposite of night is day . Time of day varies based on factors such as season, latitude, longitude and timezone.

53

Amenities	In the contexts of real estate and lodging, amenities are any tangible or intangible benefits of a property, especially those which increase the attractiveness or value of the property or which contribute to its comfort or convenience.
	Tangible amenities might include parks, swimming pools, health club facilities, party rooms, guest rooms (lodgings), theater or media rooms, bike paths, community centers, doormen, oyster bars or garages, for example.
	Intangible amenities might include a `pleasant view` or aspect, low crime rates, or a `sun-lit living room velu`, which all add to the living comforts of the property.
Technology	Technology is a broad concept that deals with human as well as other animal species` usage and knowledge of tools and crafts, and how it affects a species` ability to control and adapt to its environment. Technology is a term with origins in the Greek technología -- téchnÄ" (τĨχνη), `craft` and -logía (-λογĨ‾ α), the study of something, or the branch of knowledge of a discipline. However, a strict definition is elusive; `Technology` can refer to material objects of use to humanity, such as machines, hardware or utensils, but can also encompass broader themes, including systems, methods of organization, and techniques.
Organizational structure	An Organizational structure is a mainly hierarchical concept of subordination of entities that collaborate and contribute to serve one common aim.
	Organizations are a variant of clustered entities. An organization can be structured in many different ways and styles, depending on their objectives and ambiance.
Call for bids	A Call for bids or call for tenders or invitation to tender (ITT) (often called tender for short) is a special procedure for generating competing offers from different bidders looking to obtain an award of business activity in works, supply).
	Open tenders, open calls for tenders, or advertised tenders are open to all vendors or contractors who can guarantee performance.
War	War is a reciprocated, armed conflict between two or more non-congruous entities, aimed at reorganising a subjectively designed, geo-politically desired result. In his book, On war, Prussian military theoretician Carl Von Clausewitz calls war the `continuation of political intercourse, carried on with other means.`
	war is an interaction in which two or three or more opposing forces have a `struggle of wills`. The term is also used as a metaphor for non-military conflict, such as in the example of Class war.
Chef	A chef is a person who cooks professionally. In a professional kitchen setting, the term is used only for the one person in charge of everyone else in the kitchen; the executive chef.

`chef` is the abbreviated form of the French phrase chef de cuisine, the `chief` or `head` of a kitchen.

Kiosk

In the Mediterranean Basin and the Near East, a Kiosk is a small, separated garden pavilion open on some or all sides. Kiosks were common in Persia, India, Pakistan, and in the Ottoman Empire from the 13th century onward. Today, there are many Kiosks in and around the TopkapÄ± Palace in Istanbul, and they are still a relatively common sight in Greece.

Department

A Department is a part of a larger organization with a specific responsibility. For the division of organizations into Departments, see Departmentalization.

In particular:

· A government Department in Australia, Canada, Ireland, Sweden, Switzerland and the United States, corresponds to a ministry in other systems:

· Department (Australian government)
· Department (Swiss government)
· Departments of the United Kingdom Government
· Department (US government)

· Department (administrative division)- a geographical and administrative division within a country.
· Part of an institution such as a commercial company or a non-profit organization such as a university.

· Academic Department

· A Department store is a retail store that includes many specialized Departments such as clothing or household items.

· Part of a state or municipal government:

· Fire Department
· Police Department

· In the US military:

· `Department` is a term used by the U.S. Army, mostly prior to World War I.
· A naval Department is a section devoted to one of several major tasks.

· In the magazine context:

· Articles, essays and columns that follow a certain consistency under one topic. `

Industry

An Industry is the manufacturing of a good or service within a category. Although Industry is a broad term for any kind of economic production, in economics and urban planning Industry is a synonym for the secondary sector, which is a type of economic activity involved in the manufacturing of raw materials into goods and products.

There are four key industrial economic sectors: the primary sector, largely raw material extraction industries such as mining and farming; the secondary sector, involving refining, construction, and manufacturing; the tertiary sector, which deals with services and distribution of manufactured goods; and the quaternary sector, a relatively new type of knowledge Industry focusing on technological research, design and development such as computer programming, and biochemistry.

Activities

Activity may mean:

· Action (philosophy), in general

· the Aristotelian concept of energeia, Latinized as actus

· physical activity

· mental activity

· Activity

· Activity (UML)

· Activity, an alternative name for the game charades

· Activity, a task.

· Activity, the ability of a piece to influence the game in chess

· Activity, the rate of a catalytic reaction, such as enzyme activity, in physical chemistry and enzymology

· activity (chemistry), the effective concentration of a solute for the purposes of mass action

· activity (project management)

· activity (radioactivity), the number of radioactive decays per second

· activity (software engineering)

· activity (soil mechanics)

· activity diagram, a diagram representing activities in UML

· Activity, a board game by Piatnik

· HMS Activity, an aircraft carrier of the Royal Navy

· in military parlance, a military agency or unit (e.g. Intelligence Support Activity) .

| Product | When a product reaches the maturity stage of the product life cycle a company may choose to operate strategies to extend the life of the product. If the product is predicted to continue to be successful or an upgrade is soon to be released the company can use various methods to keep sales, else the product will be left as is to continue to the decline stage. |

Examples of extension strategies are:

· Discounted price

· Increased advertising

· Accessing another market abroad

Another strategy is added value.

This is a widely used extension strategy.

Chapter 4. Overview: Hotels, Hotels, Hotels! 59 Full-Service Hotels

Saleability	Saleability is a technical analysis term used to compare performances of different trading systems or different investments within one system. Note, it is not simply another word for profit. There are varying definitions for it, some as simple as the expected or average ratio of revenue to cost for a particular investment or trading system or `ratio of the number of winning trades or investments to the total number of trades or investments made, a number ranging from zero to 1.` Others can be complex or counter-intuitive.
Cost	In business, retail, and accounting, a Cost is the value of money that has been used up to produce something, and hence is not available for use anymore. In economics, a Cost is an alternative that is given up as a result of a decision. In business, the Cost may be one of acquisition, in which case the amount of money expended to acquire it is counted as Cost.
Percentage	In mathematics, a percentage is a way of expressing a number as a fraction of 100 (per cent meaning `per hundred`). It is often denoted using the percent sign, `%`. For example, 45% (read as `forty-five percent`) is equal to 45 / 100, or 0.45. percentages are used to express how large/small one quantity is, relative to another quantity.
Restaurant	A restaurant prepares and serves food and drink to customers. Meals are generally served and eaten on premises, but many restaurant s also offer take-out and food delivery services. restaurant s vary greatly in appearance and offerings, including a wide variety of cuisines and service models.
Order	An order in a market such as a stock market, bond market or commodity market is an instruction from a customer to a broker to buy or sell on the exchange. These instructions can be simple or complicated. There are some standard instructions for such orders.
Table	A table is both a mode of visual communication and a means of arranging data. The use of tables is pervasive throughout all communication, research and data analysis. Tables appear in print media, handwritten notes, computer software, architectural ornamentation, traffic signs and many other places.
Competition	Co-operative Competition is based upon promoting mutual survival - `everyone wins`. Adam Smith`s `invisible hand` is a process where individuals compete to improve their level of happiness but compete in a cooperative manner through peaceful exchange and without violating other people. Cooperative Competition focuses individuals/groups/organisms against the environment.
American Depositary Receipt	An American Depositary Receipt represents ownership in the shares of a non-U.S. company and trades in U.S. financial markets. The stock of many non-US companies trade on US stock exchanges through the use of American Depositary Receipts. American Depositary Receipts enable U.S. investors to buy shares in foreign companies without the hazards or inconveniences of cross-border ' cross-currency transactions.

63

Average daily rate	Average daily rate (commonly referred to as Average daily rate) is a statistical unit that is often used in the lodging industry. The number represents the average rental income per occupied room in a given time period. Average daily rate along with the property`s occupancy are the foundations for the property`s financial performance.
Construction	Construction is the most dangerous land based work sector in Europe (the fishing industry being more dangerous). In the European Union, the fatal accident rate is nearly 13 workers per 100,000 as against 5 per 100,000 for the all sector average (Source: Eurostat). In the U.S. there were 1,225 fatal occupational injuries in the Construction sector in 2001 with an incidence rate of 13.3 per 100,000 employed workers.
Monotonic function	In mathematics, a monotonic function (or monotone function) is a function which preserves the given order. This concept first arose in calculus, and was later generalized to the more abstract setting of order theory. In calculus, a function f defined on a subset of the real numbers with real values is called monotonic (also monotonically increasing or non-decreasing), if for all x and y such that $x \le y$ one has $f(x) \le f(y)$, so f preserves the order .
Internet Marketing	Internet marketing, also referred to as i-marketing, web marketing, online marketing, is the marketing of products, or, services over the Internet. The Internet has brought media to a global audience. The interactive nature of Internet marketing, both, in terms of providing instant response and eliciting responses, is a unique quality of the medium.
Employment	Employment is a contract between two parties, one being the employer and the other being the employee. An employee may be defined as: `A person in the service of another under any contract of hire, express or implied, oral or written, where the employer has the power or right to control and direct the employee in the material details of how the work is to be performed.` Black`s Law Dictionary page 471 (5th ed. 1979). In a commercial setting, the employer conceives of a productive activity, generally with the intention of generating a profit, and the employee contributes labour to the enterprise, usually in return for payment of wages.
Marketing	Marketing is a `social and managerial process by which individuals and groups obtain what they need and want through creating and exchanging products and values with others.` It is an integrated process through which companies create value for customers and build strong customer relationships in order to capture value from customers in return.

marketing is used to create the customer, to keep the customer and to satisfy the customer. With the customer as the focus of its activities, it can be concluded that marketing management is one of the major components of business management.

Dot.com bubble	The `Dot.com bubble` (or) was a speculative bubble covering roughly 1998-2001 (with a climax on March 10, 2000 with the NASDAQ peaking at 5132.52) during which stock markets in Western nations saw their equity value rise rapidly from growth in the more recent Internet sector and related fields. While the latter part was a boom and bust cycle, the Internet boom sometimes is meant to refer to the steady commercial growth of the Internet with the advent of the world wide web as exemplified by the first release of the Mosaic web browser in 1993 and continuing through the 1990s.

The period was marked by the founding (and, in many cases, spectacular failure) of a group of new Internet-based companies commonly referred to as dot-coms.

Wireless	Wireless communication is the transfer of information over a distance without the use of electrical conductors or `wires`. The distances involved may be short (a few meters as in television remote control) or long (thousands or millions of kilometers for radio communications.) When the context is clear, the term is often shortened to `wireless`.

Restaurant	A restaurant prepares and serves food and drink to customers. Meals are generally served and eaten on premises, but many restaurant s also offer take-out and food delivery services. restaurant s vary greatly in appearance and offerings, including a wide variety of cuisines and service models.
Amenities	In the contexts of real estate and lodging, amenities are any tangible or intangible benefits of a property, especially those which increase the attractiveness or value of the property or which contribute to its comfort or convenience.
	Tangible amenities might include parks, swimming pools, health club facilities, party rooms, guest rooms (lodgings), theater or media rooms, bike paths, community centers, doormen, oyster bars or garages, for example.
	Intangible amenities might include a `pleasant view` or aspect, low crime rates, or a `sun-lit living room velu`, which all add to the living comforts of the property.
Upmarket	Upmarket (or high-end) commodities are products, services or real estate targeted at high-income consumers. Examples of products would include items from Ferrari, Mercedes-Benz, Hammacher -Schlemmer, and Chanel.
	In the United States, Upmarket real estate areas are generally characterized by being within the city limits or a suburb of a major city, a high concentration of multi-million dollar homes (typically several hundred or more), high household incomes (generally a family average of $275,000 per year or more), an abundance of luxury boutiques, hotels, restaurants, vehicle dealerships, exclusive golf courses and nation wide familiarity on a first name basis without the inclusion of an anchor city or state.
Defined	In mathematics, Defined and unDefined are used to explain whether or not expressions have meaningful, sensible, and unambiguous values. Whether an expression has a meaningful value depends on the context of the expression. For example the value of 4 − 5 is unDefined if a positive integer result is required.
Program	The Program (or Project) Evaluation and Review Technique, commonly abbreviated PERT, is a model for project management designed to analyze and represent the tasks involved in completing a given project.
	PERT is a method to analyze the involved tasks in completing a given project, especially the time needed to complete each task, and identifying the minimum time needed to complete the total project.
	PERT was developed primarily to simplify the planning and scheduling of large and complex projects.

Chapter 5. Limited-Service Hotels

Chapter 5. Limited-Service Hotels

Group	In business, a group, business group, corporate group) alliance is most commonly a legal entity that is a type of conglomerate or holding company consisting of a parent company and subsidiaries. Typical examples are Adidas group or Icelandair group. In United Arab Emirates, Business group can also be knows as Trade association.
Conference	A Conference is a meeting of people that `confer` about a topic. · Academic Conference, in science and academia, a formal event where researchers present results, workshops, and other activities. · Business Conference, organized to discuss business-related matters best effected there. · News Conference, an announcement to the press (print, radio, television) with the expectation of questions, about the announced matter, following. · Settlement Conference, a meeting between the plaintiff and the respondent in lawsuit, wherein they try to settle their dispute without proceeding to trial · Conference (sports), a grouping of geographically-related teams · Conference call, in telecommunications, a `multi-party call` · Conference hall, room where Conferences are held · Football Conference, an English football league · In the Netherlands, a solo cabaret act, a type of stand-up comedy lasting one to two hours · Parent-teacher Conference, a meeting with a child`s teacher to discuss grades and school performance. · UnConference .
Business	A Business (, enterprise or firm) is a legally recognized organization designed to provide goods and/or services to consumers. Businesses are predominant in capitalist economies, most being privately owned and formed to earn profit that will increase the wealth of its owners and grow the Business itself. The owners and operators of a Business have as one of their main objectives the receipt or generation of a financial return in exchange for work and acceptance of risk.
Per diem	Per diem is Latin for `per day` or `for each day`. It usually refers to the daily rate of any kind of payment. It may also refer to a specific amount of money that an organization allows an individual to spend per day, to cover living and traveling expenses in connection with work.
Nominative determinism	Nominative determinism refers to the theory that a person`s name is given an influential role in reflecting key attributes of his job, profession, but real examples are more highly prized, the more obscure the better.
Activities	Activity may mean:

· Action (philosophy), in general
· the Aristotelian concept of energeia, Latinized as actus
· physical activity
· mental activity
· Activity
· Activity (UML)
· Activity, an alternative name for the game charades
· Activity, a task.
· Activity, the ability of a piece to influence the game in chess
· Activity, the rate of a catalytic reaction, such as enzyme activity, in physical chemistry and enzymology
· activity (chemistry), the effective concentration of a solute for the purposes of mass action
· activity (project management)
· activity (radioactivity), the number of radioactive decays per second
· activity (software engineering)
· activity (soil mechanics)
· activity diagram, a diagram representing activities in UML
· Activity, a board game by Piatnik
· HMS Activity, an aircraft carrier of the Royal Navy
· in military parlance, a military agency or unit (e.g. Intelligence Support Activity) .

Organizational structure	An Organizational structure is a mainly hierarchical concept of subordination of entities that collaborate and contribute to serve one common aim.
	Organizations are a variant of clustered entities. An organization can be structured in many different ways and styles, depending on their objectives and ambiance.
Call for bids	A Call for bids or call for tenders or invitation to tender (ITT) (often called tender for short) is a special procedure for generating competing offers from different bidders looking to obtain an award of business activity in works, supply).
	Open tenders, open calls for tenders, or advertised tenders are open to all vendors or contractors who can guarantee performance.
Investor relations	Investor relations is a strategic management responsibility that integrates finance, communication, marketing and securities law compliance to enable the most effective two-way communication between a company, the financial community, and other constituencies, which ultimately contributes to a company`s securities achieving fair valuation. (Adopted by the NIRI Board of Directors, March 2003). The term describes the department of a company devoted to handling inquiries from shareholders and investors, as well as others who might be interested in a company`s stock or financial stability.

Chapter 5. Limited-Service Hotels

Chapter 5. Limited-Service Hotels

Consumer	Consumer is a broad label for any individuals or households that use goods and services generated within the economy. The concept of a Consumer is used in different contexts, so that the usage and significance of the term may vary. Typically when business people and economists talk of Consumers they are talking about person as Consumer, an aggregated commodity item with little individuality other than that expressed in the buy/not-buy decision.
Consumer Confidence Index	The U.S. Consumer Confidence Index is an indicator designed to measure consumer confidence, which is defined as the degree of optimism on the state of the economy that consumers are expressing through their activities of savings and spending. Global consumer confidence is not measured. Country by country analysis indicates huge variance around the globe.
Demand	In economics, demand is the desire to own anything and the ability to pay for it and willigness to pay . The term demand signifies the ability or the willingness to buy a particular commodity at a given point of time. demand is also defined elsewhere as a measure of preferences that is weighted by income.
Efficient-market hypothesis	In finance, the Efficient-market hypothesis (EMH) asserts that financial markets are `informationally efficient`, stocks, bonds, or property) already reflect all known information, and instantly change to reflect new information. Therefore, according to theory, it is impossible to consistently outperform the market by using any information that the market already knows, except through luck. Information or news in the EMH is defined as anything that may affect prices that is unknowable in the present and thus appears randomly in the future.

Chapter 6. Extended-Stay Hotels

Amenities	In the contexts of real estate and lodging, amenities are any tangible or intangible benefits of a property, especially those which increase the attractiveness or value of the property or which contribute to its comfort or convenience. Tangible amenities might include parks, swimming pools, health club facilities, party rooms, guest rooms (lodgings), theater or media rooms, bike paths, community centers, doormen, oyster bars or garages, for example. Intangible amenities might include a `pleasant view` or aspect, low crime rates, or a `sun-lit living room velu`, which all add to the living comforts of the property.
Defined	In mathematics, Defined and unDefined are used to explain whether or not expressions have meaningful, sensible, and unambiguous values. Whether an expression has a meaningful value depends on the context of the expression. For example the value of 4 – 5 is unDefined if a positive integer result is required.
Suit	A suit is a set of garments crafted from the same cloth, consisting of at least a jacket and trousers. Lounge suits are the most common style of Western suit, originating in England as country wear. Other types of suit still worn today are firstly the dinner suit, part of black tie, which arose as a lounging alternative to dress coats in much the same way as the day lounge suit came to replace frock and morning coats; and secondly, rarely worn today, the morning suit.
Business	A Business (, enterprise or firm) is a legally recognized organization designed to provide goods and/or services to consumers. Businesses are predominant in capitalist economies, most being privately owned and formed to earn profit that will increase the wealth of its owners and grow the Business itself. The owners and operators of a Business have as one of their main objectives the receipt or generation of a financial return in exchange for work and acceptance of risk.
Organizational structure	An Organizational structure is a mainly hierarchical concept of subordination of entities that collaborate and contribute to serve one common aim. Organizations are a variant of clustered entities. An organization can be structured in many different ways and styles, depending on their objectives and ambiance.
Conference	A Conference is a meeting of people that `confer` about a topic.

Chapter 6. Extended-Stay Hotels

Chapter 6. Extended-Stay Hotels

· Academic Conference, in science and academia, a formal event where researchers present results, workshops, and other activities.

· Business Conference, organized to discuss business-related matters best effected there.

· News Conference, an announcement to the press (print, radio, television) with the expectation of questions, about the announced matter, following.

· Settlement Conference, a meeting between the plaintiff and the respondent in lawsuit, wherein they try to settle their dispute without proceeding to trial

· Conference (sports), a grouping of geographically-related teams

· Conference call, in telecommunications, a `multi-party call`

· Conference hall, room where Conferences are held

· Football Conference, an English football league

· In the Netherlands, a solo cabaret act, a type of stand-up comedy lasting one to two hours

· Parent-teacher Conference, a meeting with a child`s teacher to discuss grades and school performance.

· UnConference .

Organization	Management is interested in organization mainly from an instrumental point of view. For a company, organization is a means to an end to achieve its goals. Among the theories that are or have been most influential are: · Pyramids or hierarchies · Committees or juries · Matrix organizations · Ecologies A hierarchy exemplifies an arrangement with a leader who leads leaders. This arrangement is often associated with bureaucracy.
Organizational chart	An organizational chart (often called organization chart, organigram(me))) is a diagram that shows the structure of an organization and the relationships and relative ranks of its parts and positions/jobs. The term is also used for similar diagrams, for example ones showing the different elements of a field of knowledge or a group of languages. The French Encyclopédie had one of the first organizational charts of knowledge in general.
Nominative determinism	Nominative determinism refers to the theory that a person`s name is given an influential role in reflecting key attributes of his job, profession, but real examples are more highly prized, the more obscure the better.
Sale	A sale is the pinnacle activity involved in selling products or services in return for money or other compensation. It is an act of completion of a commercial activity.

A sale is completed by the seller, the owner of the goods.

American Depositary Receipt	An American Depositary Receipt represents ownership in the shares of a non-U.S. company and trades in U.S. financial markets. The stock of many non-US companies trade on US stock exchanges through the use of American Depositary Receipts. American Depositary Receipts enable U.S. investors to buy shares in foreign companies without the hazards or inconveniences of cross-border ' cross-currency transactions.
Average daily rate	Average daily rate (commonly referred to as Average daily rate) is a statistical unit that is often used in the lodging industry. The number represents the average rental income per occupied room in a given time period. Average daily rate along with the property`s occupancy are the foundations for the property`s financial performance.
Activities	Activity may mean: · Action (philosophy), in general · the Aristotelian concept of energeia, Latinized as actus · physical activity · mental activity · Activity · Activity (UML) · Activity, an alternative name for the game charades · Activity, a task. · Activity, the ability of a piece to influence the game in chess · Activity, the rate of a catalytic reaction, such as enzyme activity, in physical chemistry and enzymology · activity (chemistry), the effective concentration of a solute for the purposes of mass action · activity (project management) · activity (radioactivity), the number of radioactive decays per second · activity (software engineering) · activity (soil mechanics) · activity diagram, a diagram representing activities in UML · Activity, a board game by Piatnik · HMS Activity, an aircraft carrier of the Royal Navy · in military parlance, a military agency or unit (e.g. Intelligence Support Activity) .
Competition	Co-operative Competition is based upon promoting mutual survival - `everyone wins`. Adam Smith`s `invisible hand` is a process where individuals compete to improve their level of happiness but compete in a cooperative manner through peaceful exchange and without violating other people. Cooperative Competition focuses individuals/groups/organisms against the environment.

Chapter 6. Extended-Stay Hotels

Chapter 6. Extended-Stay Hotels

Anecdotal value	In economics, Anecdotal value refers to the primarily social and political value of an anecdote or anecdotal evidence in promoting understanding of a social, cultural, in the last several decades the evaluation of anecdotes has received sustained academic scrutiny from economists and scholars such as S.G. Checkland (on David Ricardo), Steven Novella, Hollis Robbins, R. Charleton, Kwamena Kwansah-Aidoo, and others; these academics seek to quantify the value inherent in the deployment of anecdotes. More recently, economists studying choice models have begun assessing Anecdotal value in the context of framing; Kahneman and Tversky suggest that choice models may be contingent on stories or anecdotes that frame or influence choice.
Revpar	RevPAR, is an important metric relevant to the hotel industry. Often it is utilized as a primary statistic indicating the overall financial performance of a property.
	Note that RevPAR numbers represent a measure of performance in terms relative to a property`s past results, and especially in comparison to competitors within a custom defined market, trading area, or DMA. Also, comparisons are usually best considered between hotels of the same type, or with target customers.
Safety	Safety is the state of being `safe`, the condition of being protected against physical, social, spiritual, financial, political, emotional, occupational, psychological, educational or other types or consequences of failure, damage, error, accidents, harm or any other event which could be considered non-desirable. This can take the form of being protected from the event or from exposure to something that causes health or economical losses. It can include protection of people or of possessions.
September	September Â·) is the ninth month of the year in the Gregorian Calendar and one of four Gregorian months with 30 days.
	In Latin, septem means `seven` and septimus means `seventh`; September was in fact the seventh month of the Roman calendar until 153 BC, when there was a calendar reform from the month of the Ides of March to the Kalends, or January 1.
	September marks the beginning of the ecclesiastical year in the Eastern Orthodox Church.
Terrorism	Terrorism, according to the Oxford English Dictionary is `A policy intended to strike with terror those against whom it is adopted; the employment of methods of intimidation; the fact of terrorizing or condition of being terrorized.` At present, there is no internationally agreed upon definition of terrorism. Common definitions of terrorism refer only to those acts which are intended to create fear (terror), (2) are perpetrated for an ideological goal (as opposed to a materialistic goal or a lone attack), and (3) deliberately target (or disregard the safety of) non-combatants. Some definitions also include acts of unlawful violence or unconventional warfare.
Arrestee Drug Abuse Monitoring	Arrestee Drug Abuse Monitoring, was a survey conducted by the U.S. Department of Justice to gauge the prevalence of alcohol and illegal drug use among prior arrestees. It was a reformulation of the prior Drug Use Forecasting (DUF) program, focused on five drugs in particular: cocaine, marijuana, methamphetamine, opiates, and PCP.

Participants were randomly selected from arrest records in major metropolitan areas; because no personally identifying information is taken from each record chosen, the resulting data can be correlated to arrest rates, but not to the total population of persons charged.

Arrestee Drug Abuse Monitoring began as the Drug Use Forecasting program in 1987, which tested arrestees in 13 (later 23) jurisdictions on a quarterly basis.

84

Chapter 7. Convention Hotels and Conference Centers

Group	In business, a group, business group, corporate group) alliance is most commonly a legal entity that is a type of conglomerate or holding company consisting of a parent company and subsidiaries. Typical examples are Adidas group or Icelandair group. In United Arab Emirates, Business group can also be knows as Trade association.
Conference	A Conference is a meeting of people that `confer` about a topic. · Academic Conference, in science and academia, a formal event where researchers present results, workshops, and other activities. · Business Conference, organized to discuss business-related matters best effected there. · News Conference, an announcement to the press (print, radio, television) with the expectation of questions, about the announced matter, following. · Settlement Conference, a meeting between the plaintiff and the respondent in lawsuit, wherein they try to settle their dispute without proceeding to trial · Conference (sports), a grouping of geographically-related teams · Conference call, in telecommunications, a `multi-party call` · Conference hall, room where Conferences are held · Football Conference, an English football league · In the Netherlands, a solo cabaret act, a type of stand-up comedy lasting one to two hours · Parent-teacher Conference, a meeting with a child`s teacher to discuss grades and school performance. · UnConference .
Defined	In mathematics, Defined and unDefined are used to explain whether or not expressions have meaningful, sensible, and unambiguous values. Whether an expression has a meaningful value depends on the context of the expression. For example the value of $4 - 5$ is unDefined if a positive integer result is required.
Room	A Room, in architecture, is any distinguishable space within a structure. Most typically a Room is separated by interior walls from other spaces or passageways; moreover, it is separated by an exterior wall from outdoor areas, sometimes with a door. Historically the use of Rooms dates at least to early Minoan cultures about 2200 BC, where excavations on Santorini, Greece at Akrotiri reveal clearly defined Rooms within structures.
Suit	A suit is a set of garments crafted from the same cloth, consisting of at least a jacket and trousers. Lounge suits are the most common style of Western suit, originating in England as country wear. Other types of suit still worn today are firstly the dinner suit, part of black tie, which arose as a lounging alternative to dress coats in much the same way as the day lounge suit came to replace frock and morning coats; and secondly, rarely worn today, the morning suit.

87

Chapter 7. Convention Hotels and Conference Centers

Marketing	Marketing is a `social and managerial process by which individuals and groups obtain what they need and want through creating and exchanging products and values with others.` It is an integrated process through which companies create value for customers and build strong customer relationships in order to capture value from customers in return. marketing is used to create the customer, to keep the customer and to satisfy the customer. With the customer as the focus of its activities, it can be concluded that marketing management is one of the major components of business management.
Vending	A vending machine provides snacks, beverages, lottery tickets, and other products to consumers without a cashier. Items sold via these machines vary by country and region. In some countries, merchants may sell alcoholic beverages such as beer through vending machines, while other countries do not allow this practice (usually because of dram shop laws).
Business	A Business (, enterprise or firm) is a legally recognized organization designed to provide goods and/or services to consumers. Businesses are predominant in capitalist economies, most being privately owned and formed to earn profit that will increase the wealth of its owners and grow the Business itself. The owners and operators of a Business have as one of their main objectives the receipt or generation of a financial return in exchange for work and acceptance of risk.
Industry	An Industry is the manufacturing of a good or service within a category. Although Industry is a broad term for any kind of economic production, in economics and urban planning Industry is a synonym for the secondary sector, which is a type of economic activity involved in the manufacturing of raw materials into goods and products. There are four key industrial economic sectors: the primary sector, largely raw material extraction industries such as mining and farming; the secondary sector, involving refining, construction, and manufacturing; the tertiary sector, which deals with services and distribution of manufactured goods; and the quaternary sector, a relatively new type of knowledge Industry focusing on technological research, design and development such as computer programming, and biochemistry.
Call for bids	A Call for bids or call for tenders or invitation to tender (ITT) (often called tender for short) is a special procedure for generating competing offers from different bidders looking to obtain an award of business activity in works, supply). Open tenders, open calls for tenders, or advertised tenders are open to all vendors or contractors who can guarantee performance.

Chapter 7. Convention Hotels and Conference Centers

Chapter 7. Convention Hotels and Conference Centers

Customer	A Customer buyer, is usually used to refer to a current or potential buyer or user of the products of an individual or organization, called the supplier, seller, or vendor. This is typically through purchasing or renting goods or services. However, in certain contexts, the term Customer also includes by extension anyone who uses or experiences the services of another.
Professional	A professional is a member of a vocation founded upon specialised educational training.

The word professional traditionally means a person who has obtained a degree in a professional field. The term professional is used more generally to denote a white collar working person, or a person who performs commercially in a field typically reserved for hobbyists or amateurs. |
| Organizational structure | An Organizational structure is a mainly hierarchical concept of subordination of entities that collaborate and contribute to serve one common aim.

Organizations are a variant of clustered entities. An organization can be structured in many different ways and styles, depending on their objectives and ambiance. |
| Classroom | A classroom is a room in which teaching or learning activities can take place. classrooms are found in educational institutions of all kinds, including public and private schools, corporations, and religious and humanitarian organizations. The classroom attempts to provide a safe space where learning can take place uninterrupted by other distractions. |
| Organization | Management is interested in organization mainly from an instrumental point of view. For a company, organization is a means to an end to achieve its goals.

Among the theories that are or have been most influential are:

· Pyramids or hierarchies
· Committees or juries
· Matrix organizations
· Ecologies

A hierarchy exemplifies an arrangement with a leader who leads leaders. This arrangement is often associated with bureaucracy. |
| Organizational chart | An organizational chart (often called organization chart, organigram(me))) is a diagram that shows the structure of an organization and the relationships and relative ranks of its parts and positions/jobs. The term is also used for similar diagrams, for example ones showing the different elements of a field of knowledge or a group of languages. The French Encyclopédie had one of the first organizational charts of knowledge in general. |
| Sale | A sale is the pinnacle activity involved in selling products or services in return for money or other compensation. It is an act of completion of a commercial activity. |

Chapter 7. Convention Hotels and Conference Centers

A sale is completed by the seller, the owner of the goods.

Time	Time is a component of the measuring system used to sequence events, to compare the durations of events and the intervals between them, and to quantify the motions of objects. Time has been a major subject of religion, philosophy, and science, but defining it in a non-controversial manner applicable to all fields of study has consistently eluded the greatest scholars. In physics and other sciences, Time is considered one of the few fundamental quantities.
Technology	Technology is a broad concept that deals with human as well as other animal species` usage and knowledge of tools and crafts, and how it affects a species` ability to control and adapt to its environment. Technology is a term with origins in the Greek technología -- téchnÄ" (τĺχνη), `craft` and -logía (-λογî¯ α), the study of something, or the branch of knowledge of a discipline. However, a strict definition is elusive; `Technology` can refer to material objects of use to humanity, such as machines, hardware or utensils, but can also encompass broader themes, including systems, methods of organization, and techniques.
Amenities	In the contexts of real estate and lodging, amenities are any tangible or intangible benefits of a property, especially those which increase the attractiveness or value of the property or which contribute to its comfort or convenience. Tangible amenities might include parks, swimming pools, health club facilities, party rooms, guest rooms (lodgings), theater or media rooms, bike paths, community centers, doormen, oyster bars or garages, for example. Intangible amenities might include a `pleasant view` or aspect, low crime rates, or a `sun-lit living room velu`, which all add to the living comforts of the property.
Taxes	To tax is to impose a financial charge or other levy upon an individual or legal entity by a state or the functional equivalent of a state. Taxes are also imposed by many subnational entities. Taxes consist of direct tax or indirect tax, and may be paid in money or as its labour equivalent .
DMAI	DMAI (DMAI) is a professional organization representing destination marketing organizations and convention and visitor bureaus worldwide. As the world`s largest resource for official destination marketing organizations (DMOs), DMAI represents over 1,500 professionals from 658+ destination marketing organizations in more than 25 countries.

Chapter 7. Convention Hotels and Conference Centers

	They provide members -- professionals, industry partners, students and educators -- with educational resources, networking opportunities and marketing benefits available worldwide.
Destination Marketing Association International	Destination Marketing Association International is a professional organization representing destination marketing organizations and convention and visitor bureaus worldwide.
	As the world`s largest resource for official destination marketing organizations (DMOs), Destination Marketing Association International represents over 1,500 professionals from 658+ destination marketing organizations in more than 25 countries.
	They provide members -- professionals, industry partners, students and educators -- with educational resources, networking opportunities and marketing benefits available worldwide.
Construction	Construction is the most dangerous land based work sector in Europe (the fishing industry being more dangerous). In the European Union, the fatal accident rate is nearly 13 workers per 100,000 as against 5 per 100,000 for the all sector average (Source: Eurostat).
	In the U.S. there were 1,225 fatal occupational injuries in the Construction sector in 2001 with an incidence rate of 13.3 per 100,000 employed workers.
Competition	Co-operative Competition is based upon promoting mutual survival - `everyone wins`. Adam Smith`s `invisible hand` is a process where individuals compete to improve their level of happiness but compete in a cooperative manner through peaceful exchange and without violating other people. Cooperative Competition focuses individuals/groups/organisms against the environment.
Cost	In business, retail, and accounting, a Cost is the value of money that has been used up to produce something, and hence is not available for use anymore. In economics, a Cost is an alternative that is given up as a result of a decision. In business, the Cost may be one of acquisition, in which case the amount of money expended to acquire it is counted as Cost.
Wireless	Wireless communication is the transfer of information over a distance without the use of electrical conductors or `wires`. The distances involved may be short (a few meters as in television remote control) or long (thousands or millions of kilometers for radio communications.) When the context is clear, the term is often shortened to `wireless`.
Trend	A trend is a line of general direction of movement, a prevaling tendency of inclination, a style or preference, a line of development, `trend` is a synonym to `tendency`.
	A fad is a practice or interest followed for a time with exaggerated zeal.

95

Chapter 7. Convention Hotels and Conference Centers

E-commerce

Electronic commerce, commonly known as (electronic marketing) e-Commerce or eCommerce, consists of the buying and selling of products or services over electronic systems such as the Internet and other computer networks. The amount of trade conducted electronically has grown extraordinarily with widespread Internet usage. The use of commerce is conducted in this way, spurring and drawing on innovations in electronic funds transfer, supply chain management, Internet marketing, online transaction processing, electronic data interchange (EDI), inventory management systems, and automated data collection systems.

Meeting

In a Meeting, two or more people come together for the purpose of discussing a (usually) predetermined topic such as business or community event planning, often in a formal setting.

In addition to coming together physically (in real life, face to face), communication lines and equipment can also be set up to have a discussion between people at different locations, e.g. a conference call or an e-Meeting.

In organizations, Meetings are an important vehicle for personal contact.

Chapter 8. Resorts, Timeshares, and Condo-Hotels

Need for achievement	Need for achievement (N-Ach) refers to an individual`s desire for significant accomplishment, mastering of skills, control, David McClelland. Need for achievement is related to the difficulty of tasks people choose to undertake.
Timeshare	A Timeshare is a form of ownership or right to the use of a property, in which multiple parties hold rights to use the property, and each sharer is allotted a period of time (typically one week, and almost always the same time every year) in which they may use the property. Units may be on a part-ownership or lease/`right to use` basis, in which the sharer holds no claim to ownership of the property.
Defined	In mathematics, Defined and unDefined are used to explain whether or not expressions have meaningful, sensible, and unambiguous values. Whether an expression has a meaningful value depends on the context of the expression. For example the value of $4 - 5$ is unDefined if a positive integer result is required.
Ownership	Ownership is the state or fact of exclusive rights and control over property, which may be an object, land/real estate or intellectual property. An ownership right is also referred to as title. The concept of ownership has existed for thousands of years and in all cultures.
Season	A season is a division of the year, marked by changes in weather. season s result from the yearly revolution of the Earth around the Sun and the tilt of the Earth`s axis relative to the plane of revolution. In temperate and polar regions, the season s are marked by changes in the intensity of sunlight that reaches the Earth`s surface, variations of which may cause animals to go into hibernation or to migrate, and plants to be dormant.
Condominium	A Condominium, is the form of housing tenure and other real property where a specified part of a piece of real estate (usually of an apartment house) is individually owned while use of and access to common facilities in the piece such as hallways, heating system, elevators, exterior areas is executed under legal rights associated with the individual ownership and controlled by the association of owners that jointly represent ownership of the whole piece. Colloquially, the term is often used to refer to the unit itself in place of the word `apartment`. A Condominium may be simply defined as an `apartment` that the resident `owns` as opposed to rents.
Point	In typography, a point is the smallest unit of measure, being a subdivision of the larger pica. It is commonly abbreviated as pt. The traditional printer`s point, from the era of hot metal typesetting and presswork, varied between 0.18 and 0.4 mm depending on various definitions of the foot. Today, the traditional point has been supplanted by the desktop publishing point (also called the PostScript point), which has been rounded to an even 72 points to the inch (1 point = $^{127}/_{360}$ mm $\approx$ 0.353 mm).

Chapter 8. Resorts, Timeshares, and Condo-Hotels

Maxima	In mathematics, maxima and minima, known collectively as extrema (singular: extremum), are the largest value (maximum) or smallest value (minimum), that a function takes in a point either within a given neighbourhood (local extremum) or on the function domain in its entirety (global extremum).
	Throughout, a Point refers to an input (x), while a value refers to an output (y): one distinguishing between the maximum value and the point (or points) at which it occurs.
	A real-valued function f defined on the real line is said to have a local (or relative) maximum point at the point x^*, if there exists some $\varepsilon > 0$, such that $f(x^*) \geq f(x)$ when $\lvert x - x^* \rvert < \varepsilon$.
Department	A Department is a part of a larger organization with a specific responsibility. For the division of organizations into Departments, see Departmentalization.
	In particular:
	· A government Department in Australia, Canada, Ireland, Sweden, Switzerland and the United States, corresponds to a ministry in other systems:
	· Department (Australian government) · Department (Swiss government) · Departments of the United Kingdom Government · Department (US government)
	· Department (administrative division)- a geographical and administrative division within a country. · Part of an institution such as a commercial company or a non-profit organization such as a university.
	· Academic Department
	· A Department store is a retail store that includes many specialized Departments such as clothing or household items.
	· Part of a state or municipal government:

101

· Fire Department
· Police Department

· In the US military:

· `Department` is a term used by the U.S. Army, mostly prior to World War I.
· A naval Department is a section devoted to one of several major tasks.

· In the magazine context:

· Articles, essays and columns that follow a certain consistency under one topic. `

Organizational structure	An Organizational structure is a mainly hierarchical concept of subordination of entities that collaborate and contribute to serve one common aim.
	Organizations are a variant of clustered entities. An organization can be structured in many different ways and styles, depending on their objectives and ambiance.
Organization	Management is interested in organization mainly from an instrumental point of view. For a company, organization is a means to an end to achieve its goals.
	Among the theories that are or have been most influential are:
	· Pyramids or hierarchies · Committees or juries · Matrix organizations · Ecologies
	A hierarchy exemplifies an arrangement with a leader who leads leaders. This arrangement is often associated with bureaucracy.

Organizational chart	An organizational chart (often called organization chart, organigram(me))) is a diagram that shows the structure of an organization and the relationships and relative ranks of its parts and positions/jobs. The term is also used for similar diagrams, for example ones showing the different elements of a field of knowledge or a group of languages. The French Encyclopédie had one of the first organizational charts of knowledge in general.
Activities	Activity may mean: · Action (philosophy), in general · the Aristotelian concept of energeia, Latinized as actus · physical activity · mental activity · Activity · Activity (UML) · Activity, an alternative name for the game charades · Activity, a task. · Activity, the ability of a piece to influence the game in chess · Activity, the rate of a catalytic reaction, such as enzyme activity, in physical chemistry and enzymology · activity (chemistry), the effective concentration of a solute for the purposes of mass action · activity (project management) · activity (radioactivity), the number of radioactive decays per second · activity (software engineering) · activity (soil mechanics) · activity diagram, a diagram representing activities in UML · Activity, a board game by Piatnik · HMS Activity, an aircraft carrier of the Royal Navy · in military parlance, a military agency or unit (e.g. Intelligence Support Activity) .
Sale	A sale is the pinnacle activity involved in selling products or services in return for money or other compensation. It is an act of completion of a commercial activity. A sale is completed by the seller, the owner of the goods.
Competition	Co-operative Competition is based upon promoting mutual survival - `everyone wins`. Adam Smith`s `invisible hand` is a process where individuals compete to improve their level of happiness but compete in a cooperative manner through peaceful exchange and without violating other people. Cooperative Competition focuses individuals/groups/organisms against the environment.
Social	The term social refers to a characteristic of living organisms (humans in particular, though biologists also apply the term to populations of other animals). It always refers to the interaction of organisms with other organisms and to their collective co-existence, irrespective of whether they are aware of it or not, and irrespective of whether the interaction is voluntary or involuntary.

105

In the absence of agreement about its meaning, the term `ps` is used in many different senses and regarded as a [[]], referringse among other things to:

· Attitudes, orientations, or behaviours which take the interests, intentions, or needs of other people into account (in contrast to anti-social behaviour);has played some role in defining the idea or the principle. For instance terms like social realism, social justice, social constructivism, social psychology and social capital imply that there is some social process involved or considered, a process that is not there in regular, `non-social`, realism, justice, constructivism, psychology, or capital.

Social issues

Social issues are matters which directly or indirectly affect many or all members of a society and are considered to be problems, controversies related to moral values, or both.

Social issues include poverty, violence, pollution, injustice, suppression of human rights, discrimination, and crime, as well as abortion, gay marriage, gun control, and religion, to name a few.

Social issues are related to the fabric of the community, including conflicts among the interests of community members, and lie beyond the control of any one individual.

Anecdotal value

In economics, Anecdotal value refers to the primarily social and political value of an anecdote or anecdotal evidence in promoting understanding of a social, cultural, in the last several decades the evaluation of anecdotes has received sustained academic scrutiny from economists and scholars such as S.G. Checkland (on David Ricardo), Steven Novella, Hollis Robbins, R. Charleton, Kwamena Kwansah-Aidoo, and others; these academics seek to quantify the value inherent in the deployment of anecdotes. More recently, economists studying choice models have begun assessing Anecdotal value in the context of framing; Kahneman and Tversky suggest that choice models may be contingent on stories or anecdotes that frame or influence choice.

Recession

In economics, a Recession is a general slowdown in economic activity over a sustained period of time, or a business cycle contraction. During Recession s, many macroeconomic indicators vary in a similar way. Production as measured by Gross Domestic Product (GDP), employment, investment spending, capacity utilization, household incomes and business profits all fall during Recession s.

Safety

Safety is the state of being `safe`, the condition of being protected against physical, social, spiritual, financial, political, emotional, occupational, psychological, educational or other types or consequences of failure, damage, error, accidents, harm or any other event which could be considered non-desirable. This can take the form of being protected from the event or from exposure to something that causes health or economical losses. It can include protection of people or of possessions.

Chapter 8. Resorts, Timeshares, and Condo-Hotels

September	September Â·) is the ninth month of the year in the Gregorian Calendar and one of four Gregorian months with 30 days.
	In Latin, septem means `seven` and septimus means `seventh`; September was in fact the seventh month of the Roman calendar until 153 BC, when there was a calendar reform from the month of the Ides of March to the Kalends, or January 1.
	September marks the beginning of the ecclesiastical year in the Eastern Orthodox Church.
Business	A Business (, enterprise or firm) is a legally recognized organization designed to provide goods and/or services to consumers. Businesses are predominant in capitalist economies, most being privately owned and formed to earn profit that will increase the wealth of its owners and grow the Business itself. The owners and operators of a Business have as one of their main objectives the receipt or generation of a financial return in exchange for work and acceptance of risk.
Popularity	Popularity is the quality of being well-liked or common. popularity figures are an important part of many people`s personal value systems, and forms a vital component of success in people-oriented fields such as Management, politics, Entertainment Industry among others.
	Borrowed from the Latin popularis in 1490, originally meant common or `belonging to the people`.
Terrorism	Terrorism, according to the Oxford English Dictionary is `A policy intended to strike with terror those against whom it is adopted; the employment of methods of intimidation; the fact of terrorizing or condition of being terrorized.` At present, there is no internationally agreed upon definition of terrorism. Common definitions of terrorism refer only to those acts which are intended to create fear (terror), (2) are perpetrated for an ideological goal (as opposed to a materialistic goal or a lone attack), and (3) deliberately target (or disregard the safety of) non-combatants. Some definitions also include acts of unlawful violence or unconventional warfare.
Accounting	Accountancy is the art of communicating financial information about a business entity to users such as shareholders and managers. The communication is generally in the form of financial statements that show in money terms the economic resources under the control of management.
	Accounting is called `the language of business` because it is the vehicle for reporting financial information about a buisness entity to many different groups of people.
Cost	In business, retail, and accounting, a Cost is the value of money that has been used up to produce something, and hence is not available for use anymore. In economics, a Cost is an alternative that is given up as a result of a decision. In business, the Cost may be one of acquisition, in which case the amount of money expended to acquire it is counted as Cost.

Chapter 8. Resorts, Timeshares, and Condo-Hotels

Equity	Equity, in finance and accounting, is the residual claim or interest of the most junior class of investors in an asset, after all liabilities are paid. If valuations placed on assets do not exceed liabilities, negative Equity exists. In an accounting context, Shareholders` Equity (or stockholders` Equity, shareholders` funds, shareholders` capital or similar terms) represents the remaining interest in assets of a company, spread among individual shareholders of common or preferred stock.
Construction	Construction is the most dangerous land based work sector in Europe (the fishing industry being more dangerous). In the European Union, the fatal accident rate is nearly 13 workers per 100,000 as against 5 per 100,000 for the all sector average (Source: Eurostat). In the U.S. there were 1,225 fatal occupational injuries in the Construction sector in 2001 with an incidence rate of 13.3 per 100,000 employed workers.
Construction loan	In the broadest sense of the term, a Construction loan is any loan where the proceeds are used to finance construction of some kind. In the United States Financial Services industry however, the term is used to describe a genre of loans designed for construction and containing features such as interest reserves, where repayment ability may be based on something that can only occour when the project is built. Thus the defining features of these loans are special monitoring and guidelines above normal loan guidelines to ensure that the project is completed so that repayment can begin to take place.
Floating interest rate	A Floating interest rate, also known as a variable rate or adjustable rate, refers to any type of debt instrument, such as a loan, bond, mortgage, that does not have a fixed rate of interest over the life of the instrument. Such debt typically uses an index or other base rate for establishing the interest rate for each relevant period. One of the most common rates to use as the basis for applying interest rates is the London Inter-bank Offered Rate, or LIBOR (the rates at which large banks lend to each other).
Saleability	Saleability is a technical analysis term used to compare performances of different trading systems or different investments within one system. Note, it is not simply another word for profit. There are varying definitions for it, some as simple as the expected or average ratio of revenue to cost for a particular investment or trading system or `ratio of the number of winning trades or investments to the total number of trades or investments made, a number ranging from zero to 1.` Others can be complex or counter-intuitive.
Elawyering	The term Elawyering or e-lawyering is a neologism used to refer to the practice of law over the Internet, in a way more expansive than a mere legal related internet advertisement for a service, lawyer, Elawyering initiatives have been undertaken by the American Bar Association in order to reach a `latent market` of lower and middle class citizens in need of legal services. Lawyers practicing law online are also referred to as `virtual lawyers` and practice from virtual law offices.

Regulatory	Regulation refers to `controlling human or societal behaviour by rules or restrictions.` Regulation can take many forms: legal restrictions promulgated by a government authority, self-regulation, social regulation (e.g. norms), co-regulation and market regulation. One can consider regulation as actions of conduct imposing sanctions (such as a fine.) This action of administrative law, or implementing regulatory law, may be contrasted with statutory or case law.
Stereotype	A stereotype is a commonly held public belief about specific social groups, based on some prior assumptions.

Chapter 9. Overview: Profit-Making (Commercial) Foodservices

Upmarket	Upmarket (or high-end) commodities are products, services or real estate targeted at high-income consumers. Examples of products would include items from Ferrari, Mercedes-Benz, Hammacher -Schlemmer, and Chanel.
	In the United States, Upmarket real estate areas are generally characterized by being within the city limits or a suburb of a major city, a high concentration of multi-million dollar homes (typically several hundred or more), high household incomes (generally a family average of $275,000 per year or more), an abundance of luxury boutiques, hotels, restaurants, vehicle dealerships, exclusive golf courses and nation wide familiarity on a first name basis without the inclusion of an anchor city or state.
Defined	In mathematics, Defined and unDefined are used to explain whether or not expressions have meaningful, sensible, and unambiguous values. Whether an expression has a meaningful value depends on the context of the expression. For example the value of $4 - 5$ is unDefined if a positive integer result is required.
Restaurant	A restaurant prepares and serves food and drink to customers. Meals are generally served and eaten on premises, but many restaurant s also offer take-out and food delivery services. restaurant s vary greatly in appearance and offerings, including a wide variety of cuisines and service models.
Call for bids	A Call for bids or call for tenders or invitation to tender (ITT) (often called tender for short) is a special procedure for generating competing offers from different bidders looking to obtain an award of business activity in works, supply).
	Open tenders, open calls for tenders, or advertised tenders are open to all vendors or contractors who can guarantee performance.
Multiple comparisons	In statistics, the multiple comparisons (or `multiple testing`) problem occurs when one considers a set, of statistical inferences simultaneously. Errors in inference, including confidence intervals that fail to include their corresponding population parameters, or hypothesis tests that incorrectly reject the null hypothesis, are more likely to occur when one considers the family as a whole. Several statistical techniques have been developed to prevent this from happening, allowing significance levels for single and multiple comparisons to be directly compared.
Bars	BARS (or `split sphere`) is a high-pressure high-temperature apparatus usually used for growing or processing minerals, especially diamond. The name is a transliteration of a Russian abbreviation Ð'Ð Ð Ð¡ = Ð'ÐµÑ Ð¿Ñ€ÐµÑ Ñ Ð¾Ð²Ð°Ñ Ð Ð¿¿Ð¿Ð Ñ€Ð°Ñ Ñ‚,ÑƒÑ€Ð° Ð²Ñ‹Ñ Ð¾Ðº¾Ð³¾Ð³¾ Ð´Ð°²Ð»ÐµÐ½Ð Ñ `Ð Ð °Ð·Ñ€ÐµÐ·Ð½Ð°Ñ Ñ Ñ„ÐµÑ€Ð°° . Typical pressures and temperatures achievable with BARS are 10 GPa and 2500 °C.

115

Chapter 9. Overview: Profit-Making (Commercial) Foodservices

	The BARS technology was invented around 1989-1991 by the scientists from the Institute of Geology and Geophysics of the Siberian branch of the Academy of Sciences of the USSR. In the center of the device, there is a ceramic cylindrical reaction cell of about 2 cm^3 in size.
Business	A Business (, enterprise or firm) is a legally recognized organization designed to provide goods and/or services to consumers. Businesses are predominant in capitalist economies, most being privately owned and formed to earn profit that will increase the wealth of its owners and grow the Business itself. The owners and operators of a Business have as one of their main objectives the receipt or generation of a financial return in exchange for work and acceptance of risk.
Career	Career is a term defined by the Oxford English Dictionary as an individual`s `course or progress through life `. It is usually considered to pertain to remunerative work (and sometimes also formal education). The etymology of the term is somewhat ironic in that it comes from the Latin word carrera, which means race .
Food and beverage	F'B is a common abbreviation in the United States and Commonwealth countries, including Hong Kong. F'B is typically the widely accepted abbreviation for `food and beverage,` which is the sector/industry that specializes in the conceptualization, the making of, and delivery of foods. The largest section of F'B employees are in restaurants and bars, including hotels, resorts, and casinos.
Industry	An Industry is the manufacturing of a good or service within a category. Although Industry is a broad term for any kind of economic production, in economics and urban planning Industry is a synonym for the secondary sector, which is a type of economic activity involved in the manufacturing of raw materials into goods and products. There are four key industrial economic sectors: the primary sector, largely raw material extraction industries such as mining and farming; the secondary sector, involving refining, construction, and manufacturing; the tertiary sector, which deals with services and distribution of manufactured goods; and the quaternary sector, a relatively new type of knowledge Industry focusing on technological research, design and development such as computer programming, and biochemistry.
Opportunities	`opportunities (Let`s Make Lots of Money)` is a song by UK synthpop duo Pet Shop Boys, released as a single in 1985 and then in 1986, gaining greater popularity in both the UK and U.S. with its second release. Written as a satire of Thatcherism and its embodiment in conspicuous consumption and yuppies in the United Kingdom during the 1980s, the song`s indirect attack on its subject matter has come to exemplify the Pet Shop Boys as ironists in their songwriting.

Chapter 9. Overview: Profit-Making (Commercial) Foodservices

Chapter 9. Overview: Profit-Making (Commercial) Foodservices

	The song was written during the Pet Shop Boys` formative years, in 1983. According to Neil Tennant, the main lyrical concept came while in a recording studio in Camden Town when Chris Lowe asked him to make up a lyric based around the line `Let`s make lots of money`.
Room	A Room, in architecture, is any distinguishable space within a structure. Most typically a Room is separated by interior walls from other spaces or passageways; moreover, it is separated by an exterior wall from outdoor areas, sometimes with a door. Historically the use of Rooms dates at least to early Minoan cultures about 2200 BC, where excavations on Santorini, Greece at Akrotiri reveal clearly defined Rooms within structures.
Table	A table is both a mode of visual communication and a means of arranging data. The use of tables is pervasive throughout all communication, research and data analysis. Tables appear in print media, handwritten notes, computer software, architectural ornamentation, traffic signs and many other places.
Planning	Planning in organizations and public policy is both the organizational process of creating and maintaining a plan; and the psychological process of thinking about the activities required to create a desired goal on some scale. As such, it is a fundamental property of intelligent behavior. This thought process is essential to the creation and refinement of a plan, or integration of it with other plans, that is, it combines forecasting of developments with the preparation of scenarios of how to react to them.
Competition	Co-operative Competition is based upon promoting mutual survival - `everyone wins`. Adam Smith`s `invisible hand` is a process where individuals compete to improve their level of happiness but compete in a cooperative manner through peaceful exchange and without violating other people. Cooperative Competition focuses individuals/groups/organisms against the environment.
Marketing	Marketing is a `social and managerial process by which individuals and groups obtain what they need and want through creating and exchanging products and values with others.` It is an integrated process through which companies create value for customers and build strong customer relationships in order to capture value from customers in return. marketing is used to create the customer, to keep the customer and to satisfy the customer. With the customer as the focus of its activities, it can be concluded that marketing management is one of the major components of business management.
Celebrity branding	Celebrity branding is a type of branding, in which a celebrity uses his or her status in society to promote a product, service or charity. Celebrity branding can take several different forms, from a celebrity simply appearing in advertisements for a product, service or charity, to a celebrity attending PR events, creating his or her own line of products or services, and/or using his or her name as a brand. The most popular forms of celebrity brand lines are for clothing and fragrances.

Chapter 9. Overview: Profit-Making (Commercial) Foodservices

Demographic	Demographics data are the characteristics of a population as used in government, marketing or opinion research). Commonly-used Demographics include sex, race, age, income, disabilities, mobility (in terms of travel time to work or number of vehicles available), educational attainment, home ownership, employment status, and even location.
Value	A personal and cultural value is a relative ethic value, an assumption upon which implementation can be extrapolated. A value system is a set of consistent values and measures that are not true. A principle value is a foundation upon which other values and measures of integrity are based.
Factor	A factor or limiting resource is a factor that controls a process, such as organism growth or species population, size, or distribution. The availability of food, predation pressure, or availability of shelter are examples of factors that could be limiting for an organism. An example of a limiting factor is sunlight in the rainforest, where growth is limited to all plants in the understory unless more light becomes available (such as in the event of a tree fall).

· Temperature
· Low amount of nutrients

· Macroelements such as carbon, water (oxygen and hydrogen), nitrogen, phosphorus, sulfur, potassium, chloride, sodium, calcium, and magnesium
· Certain trace elements which are needed in small quantities
· pH level
· Air or water pressure
· Lack of water (dryness)
· Light
· Radiation, such as UV or nuclear
· Space

Pilferage	Pilferage is the theft of part of the contents of a package. It may also include theft of the contents but leaving the package, perhaps resealed with bogus contents. Small packages can be pilfered from a larger package such as a shipping container.
Procurement	Procurement is the acquisition of goods and/or services at the best possible total cost of ownership, in the right quality and quantity, at the right time, in the right place and from the right source for the direct benefit or use of corporations, individuals, generally via a contract, or it can be the same way selection for human resource Simple Procurement may involve nothing more than repeat purchasing. Complex Procurement could involve finding long term partners - or even `co-destiny` suppliers that might fundamentally commit one organization to another.

Almost all purchasing decisions include factors such as delivery and handling, marginal benefit, and price fluctuations.

Purchasing	Purchasing refers to a business or organization attempting to acquire goods or services to accomplish the goals of the enterprise. Though there are several organizations that attempt to set standards in the Purchasing process, processes can vary greatly between organizations. Typically the word `Purchasing` is not used interchangeably with the word `procurement`, since procurement typically includes Expediting, Supplier Quality, and Traffic and Logistics (T'L) in addition to Purchasing.
Quality	Quality in business, engineering and manufacturing has a pragmatic interpretation as the non-inferiority or superiority of something. Quality is a perceptual, conditional and somewhat subjective attribute and may be understood differently by different people. Consumers may focus on the specification Quality of a product/service, or how it compares to competitors in the marketplace.
Product	When a product reaches the maturity stage of the product life cycle a company may choose to operate strategies to extend the life of the product. If the product is predicted to continue to be successful or an upgrade is soon to be released the company can use various methods to keep sales, else the product will be left as is to continue to the decline stage.
	Examples of extension strategies are:
	· Discounted price · Increased advertising · Accessing another market abroad
	Another strategy is added value.
	This is a widely used extension strategy.
Convenience	Convenience is anything that is intended to save resources (time, energy) or frustration. A Convenience store at a petrol station, for example, sells items that have nothing to do with gasoline/petrol, but it saves the consumer from having to go to a grocery store. `Convenience` is a very relative term and its meaning tends to change over time.
Standard	A technical standard is an established norm or requirement. It is usually a formal document that establishes uniform engineering or technical criteria, methods, processes and practices.
	A technical standard can also be a controlled artifact or similar formal means used for calibration.
Counter	In digital logic and computing, a Counter is a device which stores (and) the number of times a particular event or process has occurred, often in relationship to a clock signal. In practice, there are two types of Counters:

· up Counters, which increase (increment) in value
· down Counters, which decrease (decrement) in value

In electronics, Counters can be implemented quite easily using register-type circuits such as the flip-flop, and a wide variety of designs exist, e.g:

· Asynchronous (ripple) Counter - changing state bits are used as clocks to subsequent state flip-flops
· Synchronous Counter - all state bits change under control of a single clock
· Decade Counter - counts through ten states per stage
· Up-down Counter - counts both up and down, under command of a control input
· Ring Counter - formed by a shift register with feedback connection in a ring
· Johnson Counter - a twisted ring Counter
· Cascaded Counter

Each is useful for different applications. Usually, Counter circuits are digital in nature, and count in natural binary. Many types of Counter circuit are available as digital building blocks, for example a number of chips in the 4000 series implement different Counters.

Cost

In business, retail, and accounting, a Cost is the value of money that has been used up to produce something, and hence is not available for use anymore. In economics, a Cost is an alternative that is given up as a result of a decision. In business, the Cost may be one of acquisition, in which case the amount of money expended to acquire it is counted as Cost.

Regulation

Regulation is `controlling human or societal behaviour by rules or restrictions.` Regulation can take many forms: legal restrictions promulgated by a government authority, self-Regulation, social Regulation (e.g. norms), co-Regulation and market Regulation. One can consider Regulation as actions of conduct imposing sanctions (such as a fine). This action of administrative law, or implementing regulatory law, may be contrasted with statutory or case law.

Regulations

The Control of Substances Hazardous to Health regulations 2002 is a United Kingdom Statutory Instrument that stipulates general requirements on employers to protect employees and other persons from the hazards of substances used at work by risk assessment, control of exposure, health surveillance and incident planning. There are also duties on employees to take care of their own exposure to hazardous substances and prohibitions on the import of certain substances into the European Economic Area. The regulations reenacted with amendements the Control of Substances Hazardous to Work regulations 1999 and implement several European Union directives.

101

Chapter 9. Overview: Profit-Making (Commercial) Foodservices

Chapter 9. Overview: Profit-Making (Commercial) Foodservices

Safety

Safety is the state of being `safe`, the condition of being protected against physical, social, spiritual, financial, political, emotional, occupational, psychological, educational or other types or consequences of failure, damage, error, accidents, harm or any other event which could be considered non-desirable. This can take the form of being protected from the event or from exposure to something that causes health or economical losses. It can include protection of people or of possessions.

Trend

A trend is a line of general direction of movement, a prevaling tendency of inclination, a style or preference, a line of development, `trend` is a synonym to `tendency`.

A fad is a practice or interest followed for a time with exaggerated zeal.

Resources

Human beings are also considered to be Resources because they have the ability to change raw materials into valuable Resources. The term Human Resources can also be defined as the skills, energies, talents, abilities and knowledge that are used for the production of goods or the rendering of services. While taking into account human beings as Resources, the following things have to be kept in mind:

· The size of the population
· The capabilities of the individuals in that population

Many Resources cannot be consumed in their original form. They have to be processed in order to change them into more usable commodities.

Competition	Co-operative Competition is based upon promoting mutual survival - `everyone wins`. Adam Smith`s `invisible hand` is a process where individuals compete to improve their level of happiness but compete in a cooperative manner through peaceful exchange and without violating other people. Cooperative Competition focuses individuals/groups/organisms against the environment.
Menu engineering	Menu engineering Is an interdisciplinary field of study devoted to the deliberate and strategic construction of menus. It is also commonly referred to as Menu Psychology. In general, the term menu engineering is used within the hospitality industry (specifically in the context of restaurants), but can be applied to any industry that displays a list of product or service offerings for consumer choice.
Call for bids	A Call for bids or call for tenders or invitation to tender (ITT) (often called tender for short) is a special procedure for generating competing offers from different bidders looking to obtain an award of business activity in works, supply). Open tenders, open calls for tenders, or advertised tenders are open to all vendors or contractors who can guarantee performance.
Employee	Employment is a contract between two parties, one being the employer and the other being the employee. An employee may be defined as: `A person in the service of another under any contract of hire, express or implied, oral or written, where the employer has the power or right to control and direct the employee in the material details of how the work is to be performed.` Black`s Law Dictionary page 471 (5th ed. 1979). In a commercial setting, the employer conceives of a productive activity, generally with the intention of generating a profit, and the employee contributes labour to the enterprise, usually in return for payment of wages.
Habits	Habits are routines of behavior that are repeated regularly, tend to occur subconsciously, without directly thinking consciously about them. Habitual behavior sometimes goes unnoticed in persons exhibiting them, because it is often unnecessary to engage in self-analysis when undertaking in routine tasks. Habituation is an extremely simple form of learning, in which an organism, after a period of exposure to a stimulus, stops responding to that stimulus in varied manners.
Organization	Management is interested in organization mainly from an instrumental point of view. For a company, organization is a means to an end to achieve its goals. Among the theories that are or have been most influential are:

Chapter 10. Food and Beverage Operations in Hotels

· Pyramids or hierarchies
· Committees or juries
· Matrix organizations
· Ecologies

A hierarchy exemplifies an arrangement with a leader who leads leaders. This arrangement is often associated with bureaucracy.

Chef

A chef is a person who cooks professionally. In a professional kitchen setting, the term is used only for the one person in charge of everyone else in the kitchen; the executive chef.

`chef` is the abbreviated form of the French phrase chef de cuisine, the `chief` or `head` of a kitchen.

Bars

BARS (or `split sphere`) is a high-pressure high-temperature apparatus usually used for growing or processing minerals, especially diamond. The name is a transliteration of a Russian abbreviation Ð'Ð Ð Ð¡ = Ð'ÐµÑ Ð¿Ñ€ÐµÑÑ Ð¾Ð²Ð°Ñ Ð Ð¿¿Ð°Ñ€Ð°Ñ‚Ñ‚,ÑƒÑ€Ð° Ð²Ñ‹Ñ Ð¾ÐºÐ¾Ð³Ð¾ Ð´Ð°Ð²Ð»ÐµÐ½Ð¸Ñ `Ð Ð°Ð·Ñ€ÐµÐ·Ð½Ð¾Ñ Ð¡Ñ„ÐµÑ€Ð° . Typical pressures and temperatures achievable with BARS are 10 GPa and 2500 °C.

The BARS technology was invented around 1989-1991 by the scientists from the Institute of Geology and Geophysics of the Siberian branch of the Academy of Sciences of the USSR. In the center of the device, there is a ceramic cylindrical reaction cell of about 2 cm^3 in size.

Business

A Business (, enterprise or firm) is a legally recognized organization designed to provide goods and/or services to consumers. Businesses are predominant in capitalist economies, most being privately owned and formed to earn profit that will increase the wealth of its owners and grow the Business itself. The owners and operators of a Business have as one of their main objectives the receipt or generation of a financial return in exchange for work and acceptance of risk.

Industry

An Industry is the manufacturing of a good or service within a category. Although Industry is a broad term for any kind of economic production, in economics and urban planning Industry is a synonym for the secondary sector, which is a type of economic activity involved in the manufacturing of raw materials into goods and products.

There are four key industrial economic sectors: the primary sector, largely raw material extraction industries such as mining and farming; the secondary sector, involving refining, construction, and manufacturing; the tertiary sector, which deals with services and distribution of manufactured goods; and the quaternary sector, a relatively new type of knowledge Industry focusing on technological research, design and development such as computer programming, and biochemistry.

Accounting

Accountancy is the art of communicating financial information about a business entity to users such as shareholders and managers. The communication is generally in the form of financial statements that show in money terms the economic resources under the control of management.

Accounting is called `the language of business` because it is the vehicle for reporting financial information about a buisness entity to many different groups of people.

Human resource

The objective of Human resources development is to foster Human resourcefulness through enlightened and cohesive policies in education, training, health and employment at all levels, from corporate to national.

Human resource management`s objective, on the other hand, is to maximize the return on investment from the organization`s human capital and minimize financial risk. It is the responsibility of Human resource managers in a corporate context to conduct these activities in an effective, legal, fair, and consistent manner.

Human resource Management serves these key functions:

· Recruitment ' Selection
· Training and Development (People or Organization)
· Performance Evaluation and Management
· Promotions/Transfer
· Redundancy
· Industrial and Employee Relations
· Record keeping of all personal data.
· Total Rewards: Employee Benefits ' Compensation
· Confidential advice to internal `customers` in relation to problems at work
· Career development
· Competency Mapping (Competency mapping is a process an individual uses to identify and describe competencies that are the most critical to success in a work situation or work role).
· Time motion study is related to Human resource Function
· Performance Appraisal

Modern analysis emphasizes that human beings are not `commodities` or `resources`, but are creative and social beings in a productive enterprise.

Procurement

Procurement is the acquisition of goods and/or services at the best possible total cost of ownership, in the right quality and quantity, at the right time, in the right place and from the right source for the direct benefit or use of corporations, individuals, generally via a contract, or it can be the same way selection for human resource Simple Procurement may involve nothing more than repeat purchasing. Complex Procurement could involve finding long term partners - or even `co-destiny` suppliers that might fundamentally commit one organization to another.

Almost all purchasing decisions include factors such as delivery and handling, marginal benefit, and price fluctuations.

Purchasing

Purchasing refers to a business or organization attempting to acquire goods or services to accomplish the goals of the enterprise. Though there are several organizations that attempt to set standards in the Purchasing process, processes can vary greatly between organizations. Typically the word `Purchasing` is not used interchangeably with the word `procurement`, since procurement typically includes Expediting, Supplier Quality, and Traffic and Logistics (T'L) in addition to Purchasing.

Report

In writing, a report is a document characterized by information or other content reflective of inquiry or investigation, which is tailored to the context of a given situation and audience. The purpose of report s is usually to inform. However, report s may include persuasive elements, such as recommendations, suggestions, or other motivating conclusions that indicate possible future actions the report reader might take.

Reports

Written Reports are documents which present specific, focused content--often the result of an experiment, investigation, an individual or the public in general. Reports are used in government, business, education, and science.

Room

A Room, in architecture, is any distinguishable space within a structure. Most typically a Room is separated by interior walls from other spaces or passageways; moreover, it is separated by an exterior wall from outdoor areas, sometimes with a door. Historically the use of Rooms dates at least to early Minoan cultures about 2200 BC, where excavations on Santorini, Greece at Akrotiri reveal clearly defined Rooms within structures.

Cost

In business, retail, and accounting, a Cost is the value of money that has been used up to produce something, and hence is not available for use anymore. In economics, a Cost is an alternative that is given up as a result of a decision. In business, the Cost may be one of acquisition, in which case the amount of money expended to acquire it is counted as Cost.

135

Chapter 10. Food and Beverage Operations in Hotels

Cross-selling	Cross-selling is defined by the Oxford English Dictionary as `the action or practice of selling among or between established clients, markets, traders, etc.` or `that of selling an additional product or service to an existing customer`. In practice businesses define Cross-selling in many different ways. Elements that might influence the definition might include: the size of the business, the industry sector it operates within and the financial motivations of those required to define the term.
Contribution margin	In cost-volume-profit analysis, a form of management accounting, Contribution margin is the marginal profit per unit sale. It is a useful quantity in carrying out various calculations, and can be used as a measure of operating leverage.

The Total Contribution margin (TCM) is Total Revenue (TR, or Sales) minus Total Variable Cost (TVC):

TCM = TR – TVC

The Unit Contribution margin (C) is Unit Revenue (Price, P) minus Unit Variable Cost (V):

C = P – V

The Contribution margin Ratio is the percentage of Contribution over Total Revenue, which can be calculated from the unit contribution over unit price or total contribution over Total Revenue:

$$\frac{C}{P} = \frac{P - V}{P} = \frac{\text{Unit Contribution Margin}}{\text{Price}} = \frac{\text{Total Contribution Margin}}{\text{Total Revenue}}$$

For instance, if the price is $10 and the unit variable cost is $2, then the unit Contribution margin is $8, and the Contribution margin ratio is $8/$10 = 80%.

Beverage functions	In catering, beverage functions are functions where beverages are served.

One important issue of beverage functions is who pays for the drinks. There are three main scenarios:

a cash bar (a.k.a. a no-host bar)

Function attendees pay for their own drinks.

Order	An order in a market such as a stock market, bond market or commodity market is an instruction from a customer to a broker to buy or sell on the exchange. These instructions can be simple or complicated. There are some standard instructions for such orders.

| Contract | In common-law systems, the five key requirements for the creation of a Contract are: 1. offer and acceptance (agreement) 2. consideration 3. an intention to create legal relations 4. legal capacity 5. formalities |

Chapter 10. Food and Beverage Operations in Hotels

In civil-law systems, the concept of consideration is not central. In addition, for some Contracts formalities must be complied with under what is sometimes called a statute of frauds.

One of the most famous cases on forming a Contract is Carlill v. Carbolic Smoke Ball Company, decided in nineteenth-century England.

Policy

A Policy is typically described as a deliberate plan of action to guide decisions and achieve rational outcome(s). However, the term may also be used to denote what is actually done, even though it is unplanned.

The term may apply to government, private sector organizations and groups, and individuals.

Chapter 11. Upscale Restaurants

Food and beverage	F'B is a common abbreviation in the United States and Commonwealth countries, including Hong Kong. F'B is typically the widely accepted abbreviation for `food and beverage,` which is the sector/industry that specializes in the conceptualization, the making of, and delivery of foods. The largest section of F'B employees are in restaurants and bars, including hotels, resorts, and casinos.
Upmarket	Upmarket (or high-end) commodities are products, services or real estate targeted at high-income consumers. Examples of products would include items from Ferrari, Mercedes-Benz, Hammacher -Schlemmer, and Chanel. In the United States, Upmarket real estate areas are generally characterized by being within the city limits or a suburb of a major city, a high concentration of multi-million dollar homes (typically several hundred or more), high household incomes (generally a family average of $275,000 per year or more), an abundance of luxury boutiques, hotels, restaurants, vehicle dealerships, exclusive golf courses and nation wide familiarity on a first name basis without the inclusion of an anchor city or state.
Defined	In mathematics, Defined and unDefined are used to explain whether or not expressions have meaningful, sensible, and unambiguous values. Whether an expression has a meaningful value depends on the context of the expression. For example the value of 4 – 5 is unDefined if a positive integer result is required.
Restaurant	A restaurant prepares and serves food and drink to customers. Meals are generally served and eaten on premises, but many restaurant s also offer take-out and food delivery services. restaurant s vary greatly in appearance and offerings, including a wide variety of cuisines and service models.
Table	A table is both a mode of visual communication and a means of arranging data. The use of tables is pervasive throughout all communication, research and data analysis. Tables appear in print media, handwritten notes, computer software, architectural ornamentation, traffic signs and many other places.
Apprenticeship	Apprenticeship is a system of training a new generation of practitioners of a skill. Apprentices (or in early modern usage `prentices`) or protégés build their careers from Apprenticeships. Most of their training is done on the job while working for an employer who helps the apprentices learn their trade, in exchange for their continuing labour for an agreed period after they become skilled.
Organization	Management is interested in organization mainly from an instrumental point of view. For a company, organization is a means to an end to achieve its goals. Among the theories that are or have been most influential are:

141

Chapter 11. Upscale Restaurants

· Pyramids or hierarchies
· Committees or juries
· Matrix organizations
· Ecologies

A hierarchy exemplifies an arrangement with a leader who leads leaders. This arrangement is often associated with bureaucracy.

Finishing	Finishing is the procedure that some single malt Scotch whisky undergoes whereby the spirit is matured in a cask of a particular origin and then spends time in a cask of different origin. Typically, the first cask is an American oak cask formerly used to mature bourbon. The second cask is usually one that has been used to mature some sort of fortified wine, often sherry, though sometimes port, madeira, or even standard wines such as burgundy or chardonnay.
Call for bids	A Call for bids or call for tenders or invitation to tender (ITT) (often called tender for short) is a special procedure for generating competing offers from different bidders looking to obtain an award of business activity in works, supply). Open tenders, open calls for tenders, or advertised tenders are open to all vendors or contractors who can guarantee performance.
Activities	Activity may mean:

Chapter 11. Upscale Restaurants

101

Chapter 11. Upscale Restaurants

· Action (philosophy), in general
· the Aristotelian concept of energeia, Latinized as actus
· physical activity
· mental activity
· Activity
· Activity (UML)
· Activity, an alternative name for the game charades
· Activity, a task.
· Activity, the ability of a piece to influence the game in chess
· Activity, the rate of a catalytic reaction, such as enzyme activity, in physical chemistry and enzymology
· activity (chemistry), the effective concentration of a solute for the purposes of mass action
· activity (project management)
· activity (radioactivity), the number of radioactive decays per second
· activity (software engineering)
· activity (soil mechanics)
· activity diagram, a diagram representing activities in UML
· Activity, a board game by Piatnik
· HMS Activity, an aircraft carrier of the Royal Navy
· in military parlance, a military agency or unit (e.g. Intelligence Support Activity) .

Chef

A chef is a person who cooks professionally. In a professional kitchen setting, the term is used only for the one person in charge of everyone else in the kitchen; the executive chef.

`chef` is the abbreviated form of the French phrase chef de cuisine, the `chief` or `head` of a kitchen.

American Culinary Federation

The American Culinary Federation was established in 1929 and is the largest professional chefs` organization in North America.

American Culinary Federation, which was the progeny of the combined visions of three chefs` associations in New York, comprises more than 22,000 members in 230 chapters across the United States, and is known as the authority on cooking in America. Its mission is to make a positive difference for culinarians through education, apprenticeship and certification, while creating a fraternal bond of respect and integrity among culinarians everywhere. One of American Culinary Federation`s defining historical moments remains the American Culinary Federation-led initiative that resulted in the upgrade of the definition of chef from domestic to professional in 1976. The American Culinary Federation is a member of the World Association of Chefs Societies.

Culinary Competitions are a vital and evolving branch of the American Culinary Federation.

Chapter 11. Upscale Restaurants

Need for achievement	Need for achievement (N-Ach) refers to an individual`s desire for significant accomplishment, mastering of skills, control, David McClelland. Need for achievement is related to the difficulty of tasks people choose to undertake.
Brown	Brown is a color term, denoting a range of composite colors produced by a mixture of orange, red or yellow with black. The term is from Old English brún, in origin for any dusky or dark shade of color. The Common Germanic adjective *brûnoz, *brûnâ meant both dark colors and a glistening or shining quality, whence burnish.

Chapter 12. Casual-Service (Midscale) Restaurants

Distributor	A Distributor is a device in the ignition system of an internal combustion engine that routes high voltage from the ignition coil to the spark plugs in the correct firing order. The first reliable battery operated ignition was developed by Dayton Engineering Laboratories Co. (Delco) and introduced in the 1910 Cadillac.
Sale	A sale is the pinnacle activity involved in selling products or services in return for money or other compensation. It is an act of completion of a commercial activity. A sale is completed by the seller, the owner of the goods.
Table	A table is both a mode of visual communication and a means of arranging data. The use of tables is pervasive throughout all communication, research and data analysis. Tables appear in print media, handwritten notes, computer software, architectural ornamentation, traffic signs and many other places.
Distribution	Distribution (or place) is one of the four elements of marketing mix. An organization or set of organizations (go-betweens) involved in the process of making a product or service available for use or consumption by a consumer or business user. The other three parts of the marketing mix are product, pricing, and promotion.
Technology	Technology is a broad concept that deals with human as well as other animal species` usage and knowledge of tools and crafts, and how it affects a species` ability to control and adapt to its environment. Technology is a term with origins in the Greek technología -- téchnÄ" (τîχνη), `craft` and -logía (-λογîᶦ α), the study of something, or the branch of knowledge of a discipline. However, a strict definition is elusive; `Technology` can refer to material objects of use to humanity, such as machines, hardware or utensils, but can also encompass broader themes, including systems, methods of organization, and techniques.
Amenities	In the contexts of real estate and lodging, amenities are any tangible or intangible benefits of a property, especially those which increase the attractiveness or value of the property or which contribute to its comfort or convenience. Tangible amenities might include parks, swimming pools, health club facilities, party rooms, guest rooms (lodgings), theater or media rooms, bike paths, community centers, doormen, oyster bars or garages, for example. Intangible amenities might include a `pleasant view` or aspect, low crime rates, or a `sun-lit living room velu`, which all add to the living comforts of the property.
Restaurant	A restaurant prepares and serves food and drink to customers. Meals are generally served and eaten on premises, but many restaurant s also offer take-out and food delivery services. restaurant s vary greatly in appearance and offerings, including a wide variety of cuisines and service models.

149

Chapter 12. Casual-Service (Midscale) Restaurants

Call for bids	A Call for bids or call for tenders or invitation to tender (ITT) (often called tender for short) is a special procedure for generating competing offers from different bidders looking to obtain an award of business activity in works, supply). Open tenders, open calls for tenders, or advertised tenders are open to all vendors or contractors who can guarantee performance.
Competitive	Competitiveness is a comparative concept of the ability and performance of a firm, sub-sector or country to sell and supply goods and/or services in a given market. Although widely used in economics and business management, the usefulness of the concept, particularly in the context of national competitiveness, is vigorously disputed by economists, such as Paul Krugman . The term may also be applied to markets, where it is used to refer to the extent to which the market structure may be regarded as perfectly competitive.
Business	A Business (, enterprise or firm) is a legally recognized organization designed to provide goods and/or services to consumers. Businesses are predominant in capitalist economies, most being privately owned and formed to earn profit that will increase the wealth of its owners and grow the Business itself. The owners and operators of a Business have as one of their main objectives the receipt or generation of a financial return in exchange for work and acceptance of risk.
Pager	A Pager (, beeper, bleep or bleeper) is a simple personal telecommunications device for short messages. A one-way numeric Pager can only receive a message consisting of a few digits, typically a phone number that the user is then expected to call. Alphanumeric Pagers are available, as well as two-way Pagers that have the ability to send and receive email, numeric pages, and SMS messages.
Planning	Planning in organizations and public policy is both the organizational process of creating and maintaining a plan; and the psychological process of thinking about the activities required to create a desired goal on some scale. As such, it is a fundamental property of intelligent behavior. This thought process is essential to the creation and refinement of a plan, or integration of it with other plans, that is, it combines forecasting of developments with the preparation of scenarios of how to react to them.
Celebrity branding	Celebrity branding is a type of branding, in which a celebrity uses his or her status in society to promote a product, service or charity. Celebrity branding can take several different forms, from a celebrity simply appearing in advertisements for a product, service or charity, to a celebrity attending PR events, creating his or her own line of products or services, and/or using his or her name as a brand. The most popular forms of celebrity brand lines are for clothing and fragrances.

Chapter 12. Casual-Service (Midscale) Restaurants

Selling	Selling is trying to make sales by persuading someone to buy one's product or service. From a management viewpoint it is thought of as a part of marketing, although the skills required are different. Sales often forms a separate grouping in a corporate structure, employing separate specialist operatives known as salesmen (singular: salesman).
Elawyering	The term Elawyering or e-lawyering is a neologism used to refer to the practice of law over the Internet, in a way more expansive than a mere legal related internet advertisement for a service, lawyer, Elawyering initiatives have been undertaken by the American Bar Association in order to reach a `latent market` of lower and middle class citizens in need of legal services. Lawyers practicing law online are also referred to as `virtual lawyers` and practice from virtual law offices.
Career	Career is a term defined by the Oxford English Dictionary as an individual's `course or progress through life `. It is usually considered to pertain to remunerative work (and sometimes also formal education). The etymology of the term is somewhat ironic in that it comes from the Latin word carrera, which means race .
Organization	Management is interested in organization mainly from an instrumental point of view. For a company, organization is a means to an end to achieve its goals. Among the theories that are or have been most influential are: · Pyramids or hierarchies · Committees or juries · Matrix organizations · Ecologies A hierarchy exemplifies an arrangement with a leader who leads leaders. This arrangement is often associated with bureaucracy.
Organizational chart	An organizational chart (often called organization chart, organigram(me))) is a diagram that shows the structure of an organization and the relationships and relative ranks of its parts and positions/jobs. The term is also used for similar diagrams, for example ones showing the different elements of a field of knowledge or a group of languages. The French Encyclopédie had one of the first organizational charts of knowledge in general.
Opportunities	`opportunities (Let's Make Lots of Money)` is a song by UK synthpop duo Pet Shop Boys, released as a single in 1985 and then in 1986, gaining greater popularity in both the UK and U.S. with its second release.

Chapter 12. Casual-Service (Midscale) Restaurants

Written as a satire of Thatcherism and its embodiment in conspicuous consumption and yuppies in the United Kingdom during the 1980s, the song's indirect attack on its subject matter has come to exemplify the Pet Shop Boys as ironists in their songwriting.

The song was written during the Pet Shop Boys' formative years, in 1983. According to Neil Tennant, the main lyrical concept came while in a recording studio in Camden Town when Chris Lowe asked him to make up a lyric based around the line `Let's make lots of money`.

Partnership	Partnerships may be formed in the legal forms of General Partnership (Offene Handelsgesellschaft, OHG) or Limited Partnership (Kommanditgesellschaft, KG). A Partnership can be formed by only one person. In the OHG, all partners are fully liable for the Partnership's debts, whereas in the KG there are general partners with unlimited liability and limited partners whose liability is restricted to their fixed contributions to the Partnership.
Profit sharing	Profit sharing, when used as a special term, refers to various incentive plans introduced by businesses that provide direct or indirect payments to employees that depend on company's profitability in addition to employees' regular salary and bonuses. In publicly traded companies these plans typically amount to allocation of shares to employees.
	The Profit sharing plans are based on predetermined economic sharing rules that define the split of gains between the company as a principal and the employee as an agent.
Cost	In business, retail, and accounting, a Cost is the value of money that has been used up to produce something, and hence is not available for use anymore. In economics, a Cost is an alternative that is given up as a result of a decision. In business, the Cost may be one of acquisition, in which case the amount of money expended to acquire it is counted as Cost.
Quality	Quality in business, engineering and manufacturing has a pragmatic interpretation as the non-inferiority or superiority of something. Quality is a perceptual, conditional and somewhat subjective attribute and may be understood differently by different people. Consumers may focus on the specification Quality of a product/service, or how it compares to competitors in the marketplace.
Resources	Human beings are also considered to be Resources because they have the ability to change raw materials into valuable Resources. The term Human Resources can also be defined as the skills, energies, talents, abilities and knowledge that are used for the production of goods or the rendering of services. While taking into account human beings as Resources, the following things have to be kept in mind:

· The size of the population
· The capabilities of the individuals in that population

Many Resources cannot be consumed in their original form. They have to be processed in order to change them into more usable commodities.

Competition

Co-operative Competition is based upon promoting mutual survival - `everyone wins`. Adam Smith`s `invisible hand` is a process where individuals compete to improve their level of happiness but compete in a cooperative manner through peaceful exchange and without violating other people. Cooperative Competition focuses individuals/groups/organisms against the environment.

101

Chapter 13. Family-Service Restaurants

Multiple comparisons	In statistics, the multiple comparisons (or `multiple testing`) problem occurs when one considers a set, of statistical inferences simultaneously. Errors in inference, including confidence intervals that fail to include their corresponding population parameters, or hypothesis tests that incorrectly reject the null hypothesis, are more likely to occur when one considers the family as a whole. Several statistical techniques have been developed to prevent this from happening, allowing significance levels for single and multiple comparisons to be directly compared.
Restaurant	A restaurant prepares and serves food and drink to customers. Meals are generally served and eaten on premises, but many restaurant s also offer take-out and food delivery services. restaurant s vary greatly in appearance and offerings, including a wide variety of cuisines and service models.
Call for bids	A Call for bids or call for tenders or invitation to tender (ITT) (often called tender for short) is a special procedure for generating competing offers from different bidders looking to obtain an award of business activity in works, supply). Open tenders, open calls for tenders, or advertised tenders are open to all vendors or contractors who can guarantee performance.
Business	A Business (, enterprise or firm) is a legally recognized organization designed to provide goods and/or services to consumers. Businesses are predominant in capitalist economies, most being privately owned and formed to earn profit that will increase the wealth of its owners and grow the Business itself. The owners and operators of a Business have as one of their main objectives the receipt or generation of a financial return in exchange for work and acceptance of risk.
Organizational structure	An Organizational structure is a mainly hierarchical concept of subordination of entities that collaborate and contribute to serve one common aim. Organizations are a variant of clustered entities. An organization can be structured in many different ways and styles, depending on their objectives and ambiance.
Conference	A Conference is a meeting of people that `confer` about a topic.

Chapter 13. Family-Service Restaurants

· Academic Conference, in science and academia, a formal event where researchers present results, workshops, and other activities.
· Business Conference, organized to discuss business-related matters best effected there.
· News Conference, an announcement to the press (print, radio, television) with the expectation of questions, about the announced matter, following.
· Settlement Conference, a meeting between the plaintiff and the respondent in lawsuit, wherein they try to settle their dispute without proceeding to trial
· Conference (sports), a grouping of geographically-related teams
· Conference call, in telecommunications, a `multi-party call`
· Conference hall, room where Conferences are held
· Football Conference, an English football league
· In the Netherlands, a solo cabaret act, a type of stand-up comedy lasting one to two hours
· Parent-teacher Conference, a meeting with a child`s teacher to discuss grades and school performance.
· UnConference .

Organization

Management is interested in organization mainly from an instrumental point of view. For a company, organization is a means to an end to achieve its goals.

Among the theories that are or have been most influential are:

· Pyramids or hierarchies
· Committees or juries
· Matrix organizations
· Ecologies

A hierarchy exemplifies an arrangement with a leader who leads leaders. This arrangement is often associated with bureaucracy.

Organizational chart

An organizational chart (often called organization chart, organigram(me))) is a diagram that shows the structure of an organization and the relationships and relative ranks of its parts and positions/jobs. The term is also used for similar diagrams, for example ones showing the different elements of a field of knowledge or a group of languages. The French Encyclopédie had one of the first organizational charts of knowledge in general.

Cost

In business, retail, and accounting, a Cost is the value of money that has been used up to produce something, and hence is not available for use anymore. In economics, a Cost is an alternative that is given up as a result of a decision. In business, the Cost may be one of acquisition, in which case the amount of money expended to acquire it is counted as Cost.

Production schedule

The production schedule is a project plan of how the production budget will be spent over a given timescale, for every phase of filmmaking.

Chapter 13. Family-Service Restaurants

· Cast
· Special Effects
· Wardrobe
· Special Equipment
· Stunts
· Extras/Silent Bits
· Props
· Make-up/Hair
· Extras/Atmosphere
· Vehicles/Animals
· Sound Effects/Music
· Production Notes

From the Breakdown Sheets the Production Manager compiles a production board using either industry standard computer software such as Movie Magic EP Scheduling, or alternatively, a free and simple to use Genie Schedule. Yet more conventional methods may rely on Microsoft Office Excel, or even paper-based systems.

From the production board the Production Manager makes-up a shooting schedule for every day of the shoot.

Prominence

In topography, prominence, also known as autonomous height, relative height, shoulder drop (in North America)), is a concept used in the categorization of hills and mountains, also known as peaks. It is a measure of the independent stature of a summit; compare topographic profile.

There are several equivalent definitions, which are satisfactory for all but Mount Everest:

· The prominence of a peak is the height of the peak`s summit above the lowest contour line encircling it and no higher summit.
· If the peak`s prominence is P metres, to get from the summit to any higher terrain one must descend at least P metres. Note that this implies that the prominence of any island or continental highpoint is equal to its elevation above sea level.

Quality

Quality in business, engineering and manufacturing has a pragmatic interpretation as the non-inferiority or superiority of something. Quality is a perceptual, conditional and somewhat subjective attribute and may be understood differently by different people. Consumers may focus on the specification Quality of a product/service, or how it compares to competitors in the marketplace.

Chapter 13. Family-Service Restaurants

Chapter 14. Quick-Service Restaurants

Career	Career is a term defined by the Oxford English Dictionary as an individual`s `course or progress through life `. It is usually considered to pertain to remunerative work (and sometimes also formal education). The etymology of the term is somewhat ironic in that it comes from the Latin word carrera, which means race .
Opportunities	`opportunities (Let`s Make Lots of Money)` is a song by UK synthpop duo Pet Shop Boys, released as a single in 1985 and then in 1986, gaining greater popularity in both the UK and U.S. with its second release. Written as a satire of Thatcherism and its embodiment in conspicuous consumption and yuppies in the United Kingdom during the 1980s, the song`s indirect attack on its subject matter has come to exemplify the Pet Shop Boys as ironists in their songwriting.  The song was written during the Pet Shop Boys` formative years, in 1983. According to Neil Tennant, the main lyrical concept came while in a recording studio in Camden Town when Chris Lowe asked him to make up a lyric based around the line `Let`s make lots of money`.
Restaurant	A restaurant prepares and serves food and drink to customers. Meals are generally served and eaten on premises, but many restaurant s also offer take-out and food delivery services. restaurant s vary greatly in appearance and offerings, including a wide variety of cuisines and service models.
Organization	Management is interested in organization mainly from an instrumental point of view. For a company, organization is a means to an end to achieve its goals. Among the theories that are or have been most influential are: · Pyramids or hierarchies · Committees or juries · Matrix organizations · Ecologies A hierarchy exemplifies an arrangement with a leader who leads leaders. This arrangement is often associated with bureaucracy.
Organizational chart	An organizational chart (often called organization chart, organigram(me))) is a diagram that shows the structure of an organization and the relationships and relative ranks of its parts and positions/jobs. The term is also used for similar diagrams, for example ones showing the different elements of a field of knowledge or a group of languages. The French Encyclopédie had one of the first organizational charts of knowledge in general.

165

Chapter 14. Quick-Service Restaurants

Activities	Activity may mean: · Action (philosophy), in general · the Aristotelian concept of energeia, Latinized as actus · physical activity · mental activity · Activity · Activity (UML) · Activity, an alternative name for the game charades · Activity, a task. · Activity, the ability of a piece to influence the game in chess · Activity, the rate of a catalytic reaction, such as enzyme activity, in physical chemistry and enzymology · activity (chemistry), the effective concentration of a solute for the purposes of mass action · activity (project management) · activity (radioactivity), the number of radioactive decays per second · activity (software engineering) · activity (soil mechanics) · activity diagram, a diagram representing activities in UML · Activity, a board game by Piatnik · HMS Activity, an aircraft carrier of the Royal Navy · in military parlance, a military agency or unit (e.g. Intelligence Support Activity) .
Stock	Economics, business, accounting, and related fields often distinguish between quantities which are stocks and those which are flows. A stock variable is measured at one specific time, and represents a quantity existing at that point in time, which may have been accumulated in the past. A flow variable is measured over an interval of time.
Accounting profit	Accounting profit is the difference between price and the costs of bringing to market whatever it is that is accounted as an enterprise (whether by harvest, extraction, manufacture) in terms of the component costs of delivered goods and/or services and any operating or other expenses. A key difficulty in measuring profit is in defining costs. Pure economic monetary profits can be zero or negative even in competitive equilibrium when accounted monetized costs exceed monetized price.
Quality	Quality in business, engineering and manufacturing has a pragmatic interpretation as the non-inferiority or superiority of something. Quality is a perceptual, conditional and somewhat subjective attribute and may be understood differently by different people. Consumers may focus on the specification Quality of a product/service, or how it compares to competitors in the marketplace.
Specification	A Specification is an explicit set of requirements to be satisfied by a material, product, or service.

Chapter 14. Quick-Service Restaurants

In engineering, manufacturing, and business, it is vital for suppliers, purchasers, and users of materials, products, or services to understand and agree upon all requirements. A Specification is a type of a standard which is often referenced by a contract or procurement document.

Cost

In business, retail, and accounting, a Cost is the value of money that has been used up to produce something, and hence is not available for use anymore. In economics, a Cost is an alternative that is given up as a result of a decision. In business, the Cost may be one of acquisition, in which case the amount of money expended to acquire it is counted as Cost.

Saleability

Saleability is a technical analysis term used to compare performances of different trading systems or different investments within one system. Note, it is not simply another word for profit. There are varying definitions for it, some as simple as the expected or average ratio of revenue to cost for a particular investment or trading system or `ratio of the number of winning trades or investments to the total number of trades or investments made, a number ranging from zero to 1.` Others can be complex or counter-intuitive.

Economies of scale

Economies of scale, in microeconomics, are the cost advantages that a business obtains due to expansion. They are factors that cause a producer`s average cost per unit to fall as scale is increased. Economies of scale is a long run concept and refers to reductions in unit cost as the size of a facility, or scale, increases.

Outsourcing

Outsourcing is subcontracting a service, such as product design or manufacturing, to a third-party company. The decision whether to outsource or to do inhouse is often based upon achieving a lower production cost, making better use of available resources, focussing energy on the core competencies of a particular business, or just making more efficient use of labor, capital, information technology or land resources. It is essentially a division of labour.

Resources

Human beings are also considered to be Resources because they have the ability to change raw materials into valuable Resources. The term Human Resources can also be defined as the skills, energies, talents, abilities and knowledge that are used for the production of goods or the rendering of services. While taking into account human beings as Resources, the following things have to be kept in mind:

· The size of the population
· The capabilities of the individuals in that population

Many Resources cannot be consumed in their original form. They have to be processed in order to change them into more usable commodities.

169

Chapter 14. Quick-Service Restaurants

Gift card	A Gift card is a restricted monetary equivalent or scrip that is issued by retailers or banks to be used as an alternative to a non-monetary gift. Highly popular, they rank as the second-most given gift by consumers in the United States (2006) and the most-wanted gift by women, and the third-most wanted by males. Gift cards have become increasingly popular as they relieve the donor of selecting a specific gift.
Technology	Technology is a broad concept that deals with human as well as other animal species' usage and knowledge of tools and crafts, and how it affects a species' ability to control and adapt to its environment. Technology is a term with origins in the Greek technología -- téchnÄ" (τι̂χνη), `craft` and -logía (-λογι̂̄ α), the study of something, or the branch of knowledge of a discipline. However, a strict definition is elusive; `Technology` can refer to material objects of use to humanity, such as machines, hardware or utensils, but can also encompass broader themes, including systems, methods of organization, and techniques.
Amenities	In the contexts of real estate and lodging, amenities are any tangible or intangible benefits of a property, especially those which increase the attractiveness or value of the property or which contribute to its comfort or convenience. Tangible amenities might include parks, swimming pools, health club facilities, party rooms, guest rooms (lodgings), theater or media rooms, bike paths, community centers, doormen, oyster bars or garages, for example. Intangible amenities might include a `pleasant view` or aspect, low crime rates, or a `sun-lit living room velu`, which all add to the living comforts of the property.
Card check	Card check is a method for American employees to organize into a labor union in which a majority of employees in a bargaining unit sign authorization forms,` stating they wish to be represented by the union. Since the National Labor Relations Act (NLRA) became law in 1935, majority sign-up has been an alternative to the National Labor Relations Board`s (NLRB) election process. There are two main differences between majority sign-up and the NLRB election process.

Chapter 15. Off-Site Catering

Business	A Business (, enterprise or firm) is a legally recognized organization designed to provide goods and/or services to consumers. Businesses are predominant in capitalist economies, most being privately owned and formed to earn profit that will increase the wealth of its owners and grow the Business itself. The owners and operators of a Business have as one of their main objectives the receipt or generation of a financial return in exchange for work and acceptance of risk.
Industry	An Industry is the manufacturing of a good or service within a category. Although Industry is a broad term for any kind of economic production, in economics and urban planning Industry is a synonym for the secondary sector, which is a type of economic activity involved in the manufacturing of raw materials into goods and products.
	There are four key industrial economic sectors: the primary sector, largely raw material extraction industries such as mining and farming; the secondary sector, involving refining, construction, and manufacturing; the tertiary sector, which deals with services and distribution of manufactured goods; and the quaternary sector, a relatively new type of knowledge Industry focusing on technological research, design and development such as computer programming, and biochemistry.
Group	In business, a group, business group, corporate group) alliance is most commonly a legal entity that is a type of conglomerate or holding company consisting of a parent company and subsidiaries. Typical examples are Adidas group or Icelandair group.
	In United Arab Emirates, Business group can also be knows as Trade association.
Restaurant	A restaurant prepares and serves food and drink to customers. Meals are generally served and eaten on premises, but many restaurant s also offer take-out and food delivery services. restaurant s vary greatly in appearance and offerings, including a wide variety of cuisines and service models.
Vending	A vending machine provides snacks, beverages, lottery tickets, and other products to consumers without a cashier. Items sold via these machines vary by country and region.
	In some countries, merchants may sell alcoholic beverages such as beer through vending machines, while other countries do not allow this practice (usually because of dram shop laws).
Conference	A Conference is a meeting of people that `confer` about a topic.

· Academic Conference, in science and academia, a formal event where researchers present results, workshops, and other activities.

· Business Conference, organized to discuss business-related matters best effected there.

· News Conference, an announcement to the press (print, radio, television) with the expectation of questions, about the announced matter, following.

· Settlement Conference, a meeting between the plaintiff and the respondent in lawsuit, wherein they try to settle their dispute without proceeding to trial

· Conference (sports), a grouping of geographically-related teams

· Conference call, in telecommunications, a `multi-party call`

· Conference hall, room where Conferences are held

· Football Conference, an English football league

· In the Netherlands, a solo cabaret act, a type of stand-up comedy lasting one to two hours

· Parent-teacher Conference, a meeting with a child`s teacher to discuss grades and school performance.

· UnConference .

Organization

Management is interested in organization mainly from an instrumental point of view. For a company, organization is a means to an end to achieve its goals.

Among the theories that are or have been most influential are:

· Pyramids or hierarchies

· Committees or juries

· Matrix organizations

· Ecologies

A hierarchy exemplifies an arrangement with a leader who leads leaders. This arrangement is often associated with bureaucracy.

Room

A Room, in architecture, is any distinguishable space within a structure. Most typically a Room is separated by interior walls from other spaces or passageways; moreover, it is separated by an exterior wall from outdoor areas, sometimes with a door. Historically the use of Rooms dates at least to early Minoan cultures about 2200 BC, where excavations on Santorini, Greece at Akrotiri reveal clearly defined Rooms within structures.

Satellite

In the context of spaceflight, a satellite is an object which has been placed into orbit by human endeavor. Such objects are sometimes called artificial satellite s to distinguish them from natural satellite s such as the Moon.

The first artificial satellite Sputnik 1, was launched by the Soviet Union in 1957.

Chapter 15. Off-Site Catering

Planning	Planning in organizations and public policy is both the organizational process of creating and maintaining a plan; and the psychological process of thinking about the activities required to create a desired goal on some scale. As such, it is a fundamental property of intelligent behavior. This thought process is essential to the creation and refinement of a plan, or integration of it with other plans, that is, it combines forecasting of developments with the preparation of scenarios of how to react to them.
Cost	In business, retail, and accounting, a Cost is the value of money that has been used up to produce something, and hence is not available for use anymore. In economics, a Cost is an alternative that is given up as a result of a decision. In business, the Cost may be one of acquisition, in which case the amount of money expended to acquire it is counted as Cost.
Foodborne illness	Foodborne illness is any illness resulting from the consumption of contaminated food. There are two types of food poisoning: food infection and food intoxication. Food infection refers to the presence of bacteria or other microbes which infect the body after consumption.
Safety	Safety is the state of being `safe`, the condition of being protected against physical, social, spiritual, financial, political, emotional, occupational, psychological, educational or other types or consequences of failure, damage, error, accidents, harm or any other event which could be considered non-desirable. This can take the form of being protected from the event or from exposure to something that causes health or economical losses. It can include protection of people or of possessions.
Activities	Activity may mean:

· Action (philosophy), in general
· the Aristotelian concept of energeia, Latinized as actus
· physical activity
· mental activity
· Activity
· Activity (UML)
· Activity, an alternative name for the game charades
· Activity, a task.
· Activity, the ability of a piece to influence the game in chess
· Activity, the rate of a catalytic reaction, such as enzyme activity, in physical chemistry and enzymology
· activity (chemistry), the effective concentration of a solute for the purposes of mass action
· activity (project management)
· activity (radioactivity), the number of radioactive decays per second
· activity (software engineering)
· activity (soil mechanics)
· activity diagram, a diagram representing activities in UML
· Activity, a board game by Piatnik
· HMS Activity, an aircraft carrier of the Royal Navy
· in military parlance, a military agency or unit (e.g. Intelligence Support Activity) .

Personal	A personal ad is an item or notice traditionally in the newspaper, similar to a classified ad but personal in nature. In British English it is also commonly known as an advert in a lonely hearts column. With its rise in popularity, the World Wide Web has also become a common medium for personals, commonly referred to as online dating.
Meeting	In a Meeting, two or more people come together for the purpose of discussing a (usually) predetermined topic such as business or community event planning, often in a formal setting. In addition to coming together physically (in real life, face to face), communication lines and equipment can also be set up to have a discussion between people at different locations, e.g. a conference call or an e-Meeting. In organizations, Meetings are an important vehicle for personal contact.
Prominence	In topography, prominence, also known as autonomous height, relative height, shoulder drop (in North America)), is a concept used in the categorization of hills and mountains, also known as peaks. It is a measure of the independent stature of a summit; compare topographic profile. There are several equivalent definitions, which are satisfactory for all but Mount Everest:

· The prominence of a peak is the height of the peak`s summit above the lowest contour line encircling it and no higher summit.

· If the peak`s prominence is P metres, to get from the summit to any higher terrain one must descend at least P metres. Note that this implies that the prominence of any island or continental highpoint is equal to its elevation above sea level.

Chapter 16. Contract Management Company Foodservices

Contract	In common-law systems, the five key requirements for the creation of a Contract are: 1. offer and acceptance (agreement) 2. consideration 3. an intention to create legal relations 4. legal capacity 5. formalities In civil-law systems, the concept of consideration is not central. In addition, for some Contracts formalities must be complied with under what is sometimes called a statute of frauds. One of the most famous cases on forming a Contract is Carlill v. Carbolic Smoke Ball Company, decided in nineteenth-century England.
Contract management	Contract management or contract administration is the management of contracts made with customers, vendors, partners, or employees. Contract management includes negotiating the terms and conditions in contracts and ensuring compliance with the terms and conditions, as well as documenting and agreeing any changes that may arise during its implementation or execution. It can be summarized as the process of systematically and efficiently managing contract creating, execution, and analysis for the purpose of maximizing financial and operational performance and minimizing risk.
Customer	A Customer buyer, is usually used to refer to a current or potential buyer or user of the products of an individual or organization, called the supplier, seller, or vendor. This is typically through purchasing or renting goods or services. However, in certain contexts, the term Customer also includes by extension anyone who uses or experiences the services of another.
Management contract	A Management contract is an arrangement under which operational control of an enterprise is vested by contract in a separate enterprise which performs the necessary managerial functions in return for a fee. Management contracts involve not just selling a method of doing things (as with franchising or licensing) but involves actually doing them. A Management contract can involve a wide range of functions, such as technical operation of a production facility, management of personnel, accounting, marketing services and training.
Career	Career is a term defined by the Oxford English Dictionary as an individual`s `course or progress through life `. It is usually considered to pertain to remunerative work (and sometimes also formal education). The etymology of the term is somewhat ironic in that it comes from the Latin word carrera, which means race .
Opportunities	`opportunities (Let`s Make Lots of Money)` is a song by UK synthpop duo Pet Shop Boys, released as a single in 1985 and then in 1986, gaining greater popularity in both the UK and U.S. with its second release. Written as a satire of Thatcherism and its embodiment in conspicuous consumption and yuppies in the United Kingdom during the 1980s, the song`s indirect attack on its subject matter has come to exemplify the Pet Shop Boys as ironists in their songwriting.

Chapter 16. Contract Management Company Foodservices

The song was written during the Pet Shop Boys` formative years, in 1983. According to Neil Tennant, the main lyrical concept came while in a recording studio in Camden Town when Chris Lowe asked him to make up a lyric based around the line `Let`s make lots of money`.

Call for bids

A Call for bids or call for tenders or invitation to tender (ITT) (often called tender for short) is a special procedure for generating competing offers from different bidders looking to obtain an award of business activity in works, supply).

Open tenders, open calls for tenders, or advertised tenders are open to all vendors or contractors who can guarantee performance.

Request for proposal

A Request for proposal is an invitation for suppliers, often through a bidding process, to submit a proposal on a specific commodity or service. A bidding process is one of the best methods for leveraging a company`s negotiating ability and purchasing power with suppliers. The Request for proposal process brings structure to the procurement decision and allows the risks and benefits to be identified clearly upfront.

Proposals

Proposals is a play by Neil Simon.

A nostalgic memory play, proposals recalls one idyllic afternoon in the summer of 1953, the last time the Hines clan gathers at its retreat in the Poconos. Clemma, the family`s housekeeper (and the story`s narrator), dreads a visit from the husband who deserted her years before.

Revenue

Revenue is a crucial part of financial analysis. A company`s performance is measured to the extent to which its asset inflows (revenues) compare with its asset outflows (expenses). Net Income is the result of this equation, but revenue typically enjoys equal attention during a standard earnings call.

Organization

Management is interested in organization mainly from an instrumental point of view. For a company, organization is a means to an end to achieve its goals.

Among the theories that are or have been most influential are:

· Pyramids or hierarchies
· Committees or juries
· Matrix organizations
· Ecologies

A hierarchy exemplifies an arrangement with a leader who leads leaders. This arrangement is often associated with bureaucracy.

Chapter 16. Contract Management Company Foodservices

Globalization	Globalization (or globalisation) describes an ongoing process by which regional economies, societies, and cultures have become integrated through a globe-spanning network of communication and exchange. The term is sometimes used to refer specifically to economic Globalization: the integration of national economies into the international economy through trade, foreign direct investment, capital flows, migration, and the spread of technology. However, Globalization is usually recognized as being driven by a combination of economic, technological, sociocultural, political, and biological factors.
Pro forma	The term pro forma is a term applied to practices that are perfunctory, pro forma earnings are those earnings of companies in addition to actual earnings calculated under the United States Generally Accepted Accounting Principles in their quarterly and yearly financial reports.
Adaptability	Adaptability (lat.: adaptÅ = fit, matching) is a feature of a system or of a process. This word has been put to use as a specialised term in different disciplines and in business operations. Word definitions of Adaptability as a specialised term differ little from dictionary definitions.
Sustainability	Sustainability, in general terms, is the ability to maintain balance of a certain process or state in any system. It is now most frequently used in connection with biological and human systems. In an ecological context, sustainability can be defined as the ability of an ecosystem to maintain ecological processes, functions, biodiversity and productivity into the future.
Regulation	Regulation is `controlling human or societal behaviour by rules or restrictions.` Regulation can take many forms: legal restrictions promulgated by a government authority, self-Regulation, social Regulation (e.g. norms), co-Regulation and market Regulation. One can consider Regulation as actions of conduct imposing sanctions (such as a fine). This action of administrative law, or implementing regulatory law, may be contrasted with statutory or case law.
Regulations	The Control of Substances Hazardous to Health regulations 2002 is a United Kingdom Statutory Instrument that stipulates general requirements on employers to protect employees and other persons from the hazards of substances used at work by risk assessment, control of exposure, health surveillance and incident planning. There are also duties on employees to take care of their own exposure to hazardous substances and prohibitions on the import of certain substances into the European Economic Area. The regulations reenacted with amendements the Control of Substances Hazardous to Work regulations 1999 and implement several European Union directives.
Resources	Human beings are also considered to be Resources because they have the ability to change raw materials into valuable Resources. The term Human Resources can also be defined as the skills, energies, talents, abilities and knowledge that are used for the production of goods or the rendering of services. While taking into account human beings as Resources, the following things have to be kept in mind: · The size of the population · The capabilities of the individuals in that population

Chapter 16. Contract Management Company Foodservices

Many Resources cannot be consumed in their original form. They have to be processed in order to change them into more usable commodities.

Chapter 17. Foodservices in Educational Organizations

Organization	Management is interested in organization mainly from an instrumental point of view. For a company, organization is a means to an end to achieve its goals. Among the theories that are or have been most influential are: · Pyramids or hierarchies · Committees or juries · Matrix organizations · Ecologies A hierarchy exemplifies an arrangement with a leader who leads leaders. This arrangement is often associated with bureaucracy.
Organizational chart	An organizational chart (often called organization chart, organigram(me))) is a diagram that shows the structure of an organization and the relationships and relative ranks of its parts and positions/jobs. The term is also used for similar diagrams, for example ones showing the different elements of a field of knowledge or a group of languages. The French Encyclopédie had one of the first organizational charts of knowledge in general.
Career	Career is a term defined by the Oxford English Dictionary as an individual`s `course or progress through life `. It is usually considered to pertain to remunerative work (and sometimes also formal education). The etymology of the term is somewhat ironic in that it comes from the Latin word carrera, which means race .
Opportunities	`opportunities (Let`s Make Lots of Money)` is a song by UK synthpop duo Pet Shop Boys, released as a single in 1985 and then in 1986, gaining greater popularity in both the UK and U.S. with its second release. Written as a satire of Thatcherism and its embodiment in conspicuous consumption and yuppies in the United Kingdom during the 1980s, the song`s indirect attack on its subject matter has come to exemplify the Pet Shop Boys as ironists in their songwriting.  The song was written during the Pet Shop Boys` formative years, in 1983. According to Neil Tennant, the main lyrical concept came while in a recording studio in Camden Town when Chris Lowe asked him to make up a lyric based around the line `Let`s make lots of money`.
Overhead	In business, Overhead, Overhead cost expense refers to an ongoing expense of operating a business (also known as Operating Expenses - rent, gas/electricity, wages etc). The term Overhead is usually used to group expenses that are necessary to the continued functioning of the business, but do not directly generate profits.

Chapter 17. Foodservices in Educational Organizations

Overhead expenses are all costs on the income statement except for direct labor and direct materials.

Cost

In business, retail, and accounting, a Cost is the value of money that has been used up to produce something, and hence is not available for use anymore. In economics, a Cost is an alternative that is given up as a result of a decision. In business, the Cost may be one of acquisition, in which case the amount of money expended to acquire it is counted as Cost.

Goal

A Goal or objective is a projected state of affairs that a person or a system plans or intends to achieve--a personal or organizational desired end-point in some sort of assumed development. Many people endeavor to reach Goals within a finite time by setting deadlines.

A desire or an intention becomes a Goal if and only if one activates an action for achieving it .

Resources

Human beings are also considered to be Resources because they have the ability to change raw materials into valuable Resources. The term Human Resources can also be defined as the skills, energies, talents, abilities and knowledge that are used for the production of goods or the rendering of services. While taking into account human beings as Resources, the following things have to be kept in mind:

· The size of the population
· The capabilities of the individuals in that population

Many Resources cannot be consumed in their original form. They have to be processed in order to change them into more usable commodities.

Program

The Program (or Project) Evaluation and Review Technique, commonly abbreviated PERT, is a model for project management designed to analyze and represent the tasks involved in completing a given project.

PERT is a method to analyze the involved tasks in completing a given project, especially the time needed to complete each task, and identifying the minimum time needed to complete the total project.

PERT was developed primarily to simplify the planning and scheduling of large and complex projects.

Satellite

In the context of spaceflight, a satellite is an object which has been placed into orbit by human endeavor. Such objects are sometimes called artificial satellite s to distinguish them from natural satellite s such as the Moon.

Chapter 17. Foodservices in Educational Organizations

The first artificial satellite Sputnik 1, was launched by the Soviet Union in 1957.

Department

A Department is a part of a larger organization with a specific responsibility. For the division of organizations into Departments, see Departmentalization.

In particular:

· A government Department in Australia, Canada, Ireland, Sweden, Switzerland and the United States, corresponds to a ministry in other systems:

· Department (Australian government)
· Department (Swiss government)
· Departments of the United Kingdom Government
· Department (US government)

· Department (administrative division)- a geographical and administrative division within a country.
· Part of an institution such as a commercial company or a non-profit organization such as a university.

· Academic Department

· A Department store is a retail store that includes many specialized Departments such as clothing or household items.

· Part of a state or municipal government:

· Fire Department
· Police Department

· In the US military:

Chapter 17. Foodservices in Educational Organizations

· `Department` is a term used by the U.S. Army, mostly prior to World War I.

· A naval Department is a section devoted to one of several major tasks.

· In the magazine context:

· Articles, essays and columns that follow a certain consistency under one topic. `

Regulation

Regulation is `controlling human or societal behaviour by rules or restrictions.` Regulation can take many forms: legal restrictions promulgated by a government authority, self-Regulation, social Regulation (e.g. norms), co-Regulation and market Regulation. One can consider Regulation as actions of conduct imposing sanctions (such as a fine). This action of administrative law, or implementing regulatory law, may be contrasted with statutory or case law.

Regulations

The Control of Substances Hazardous to Health regulations 2002 is a United Kingdom Statutory Instrument that stipulates general requirements on employers to protect employees and other persons from the hazards of substances used at work by risk assessment, control of exposure, health surveillance and incident planning. There are also duties on employees to take care of their own exposure to hazardous substances and prohibitions on the import of certain substances into the European Economic Area. The regulations reenacted with amendements the Control of Substances Hazardous to Work regulations 1999 and implement several European Union directives.

Activities

Activity may mean:

· Action (philosophy), in general
· the Aristotelian concept of energeia, Latinized as actus
· physical activity
· mental activity
· Activity
· Activity (UML)
· Activity, an alternative name for the game charades
· Activity, a task.
· Activity, the ability of a piece to influence the game in chess
· Activity, the rate of a catalytic reaction, such as enzyme activity, in physical chemistry and enzymology
· activity (chemistry), the effective concentration of a solute for the purposes of mass action
· activity (project management)
· activity (radioactivity), the number of radioactive decays per second
· activity (software engineering)
· activity (soil mechanics)
· activity diagram, a diagram representing activities in UML
· Activity, a board game by Piatnik
· HMS Activity, an aircraft carrier of the Royal Navy
· in military parlance, a military agency or unit (e.g. Intelligence Support Activity) .

Revenue	Revenue is a crucial part of financial analysis. A company's performance is measured to the extent to which its asset inflows (revenues) compare with its asset outflows (expenses). Net Income is the result of this equation, but revenue typically enjoys equal attention during a standard earnings call.
Trend	A trend is a line of general direction of movement, a prevaling tendency of inclination, a style or preference, a line of development, `trend` is a synonym to `tendency`. A fad is a practice or interest followed for a time with exaggerated zeal.
Technology	Technology is a broad concept that deals with human as well as other animal species' usage and knowledge of tools and crafts, and how it affects a species' ability to control and adapt to its environment. Technology is a term with origins in the Greek technología -- téchnÄ" (τîχνη), `craft` and -logía (-λογî¯ α), the study of something, or the branch of knowledge of a discipline. However, a strict definition is elusive; `Technology` can refer to material objects of use to humanity, such as machines, hardware or utensils, but can also encompass broader themes, including systems, methods of organization, and techniques.
Amenities	In the contexts of real estate and lodging, amenities are any tangible or intangible benefits of a property, especially those which increase the attractiveness or value of the property or which contribute to its comfort or convenience.

Chapter 17. Foodservices in Educational Organizations

Tangible amenities might include parks, swimming pools, health club facilities, party rooms, guest rooms (lodgings), theater or media rooms, bike paths, community centers, doormen, oyster bars or garages, for example.

Intangible amenities might include a `pleasant view` or aspect, low crime rates, or a `sun-lit living room velu`, which all add to the living comforts of the property.

Employment

Employment is a contract between two parties, one being the employer and the other being the employee. An employee may be defined as: `A person in the service of another under any contract of hire, express or implied, oral or written, where the employer has the power or right to control and direct the employee in the material details of how the work is to be performed.` Black`s Law Dictionary page 471 (5th ed. 1979).

In a commercial setting, the employer conceives of a productive activity, generally with the intention of generating a profit, and the employee contributes labour to the enterprise, usually in return for payment of wages.

200

Chapter 18. Food and Nutrition Services in Healthcare Facilities

Healthcare	Healthcare is rationed in the United States in various ways. Access to private health care insurance is rationed in part on price and ability to pay. Those not able to afford a health insurance policy are unable to acquire one, and sometimes insurance companies pre-screen applicants for pre-existing medical conditions and either decline to cover the applicant or apply additional price and medical coverage conditions.
Regulation	Regulation is `controlling human or societal behaviour by rules or restrictions.` Regulation can take many forms: legal restrictions promulgated by a government authority, self-Regulation, social Regulation (e.g. norms), co-Regulation and market Regulation. One can consider Regulation as actions of conduct imposing sanctions (such as a fine). This action of administrative law, or implementing regulatory law, may be contrasted with statutory or case law.
Regulations	The Control of Substances Hazardous to Health regulations 2002 is a United Kingdom Statutory Instrument that stipulates general requirements on employers to protect employees and other persons from the hazards of substances used at work by risk assessment, control of exposure, health surveillance and incident planning. There are also duties on employees to take care of their own exposure to hazardous substances and prohibitions on the import of certain substances into the European Economic Area. The regulations reenacted with amendements the Control of Substances Hazardous to Work regulations 1999 and implement several European Union directives.
Goal	A Goal or objective is a projected state of affairs that a person or a system plans or intends to achieve--a personal or organizational desired end-point in some sort of assumed development. Many people endeavor to reach Goals within a finite time by setting deadlines. A desire or an intention becomes a Goal if and only if one activates an action for achieving it .
Cost	In business, retail, and accounting, a Cost is the value of money that has been used up to produce something, and hence is not available for use anymore. In economics, a Cost is an alternative that is given up as a result of a decision. In business, the Cost may be one of acquisition, in which case the amount of money expended to acquire it is counted as Cost.
Anecdotal value	In economics, Anecdotal value refers to the primarily social and political value of an anecdote or anecdotal evidence in promoting understanding of a social, cultural, in the last several decades the evaluation of anecdotes has received sustained academic scrutiny from economists and scholars such as S.G. Checkland (on David Ricardo), Steven Novella, Hollis Robbins, R. Charleton, Kwamena Kwansah-Aidoo, and others; these academics seek to quantify the value inherent in the deployment of anecdotes. More recently, economists studying choice models have begun assessing Anecdotal value in the context of framing; Kahneman and Tversky suggest that choice models may be contingent on stories or anecdotes that frame or influence choice.

Chapter 18. Food and Nutrition Services in Healthcare Facilities

Business	A Business (, enterprise or firm) is a legally recognized organization designed to provide goods and/or services to consumers. Businesses are predominant in capitalist economies, most being privately owned and formed to earn profit that will increase the wealth of its owners and grow the Business itself. The owners and operators of a Business have as one of their main objectives the receipt or generation of a financial return in exchange for work and acceptance of risk.
Brain drain	Brain drain or human capital flight is a large emigration of individuals with technical skills or knowledge, normally due to conflict, lack of opportunity, political instability, since emigrants usually take with them the fraction of value of their training sponsored by the government. It is a parallel of capital flight which refers to the same movement of financial capital.
Community service	Community service is an act by a person that benefits the local community. People become involved in community service for many reasons: for some, serving community is an altruistic act, for others it is a punishment. community service therefore refers to projects that members of certain youth organizations, such as the Boy Scouts or Girl Scouts, Camp Fire USA, Key Club International, JROTC`s and some high school students perform.
Organization	Management is interested in organization mainly from an instrumental point of view. For a company, organization is a means to an end to achieve its goals. Among the theories that are or have been most influential are: · Pyramids or hierarchies · Committees or juries · Matrix organizations · Ecologies A hierarchy exemplifies an arrangement with a leader who leads leaders. This arrangement is often associated with bureaucracy.
Organizational chart	An organizational chart (often called organization chart, organigram(me))) is a diagram that shows the structure of an organization and the relationships and relative ranks of its parts and positions/jobs. The term is also used for similar diagrams, for example ones showing the different elements of a field of knowledge or a group of languages. The French Encyclopédie had one of the first organizational charts of knowledge in general.
Call for bids	A Call for bids or call for tenders or invitation to tender (ITT) (often called tender for short) is a special procedure for generating competing offers from different bidders looking to obtain an award of business activity in works, supply).

Chapter 18. Food and Nutrition Services in Healthcare Facilities

Open tenders, open calls for tenders, or advertised tenders are open to all vendors or contractors who can guarantee performance.

Commission

The Health and Safety Commission (HSC), was a United Kingdom non-departmental public body. The HSC was created by the Health and Safety at Work etc. Act 1974 (HSWA).

Construction

Construction is the most dangerous land based work sector in Europe (the fishing industry being more dangerous). In the European Union, the fatal accident rate is nearly 13 workers per 100,000 as against 5 per 100,000 for the all sector average (Source: Eurostat).

In the U.S. there were 1,225 fatal occupational injuries in the Construction sector in 2001 with an incidence rate of 13.3 per 100,000 employed workers.

Joint Commission on Accreditation of Healthcare Organizations

The Joint Commission, formerly the Joint Commission on Accreditation of Healthcare Organizations (JCAHO), is a private sector United States-based not-for-profit organization. The Joint Commission operates voluntary accreditation programs for hospitals and other health care organizations. The Joint Commission accredits over 17,000 health care organizations and programs in the United States.

Activities

Activity may mean:

· Action (philosophy), in general
· the Aristotelian concept of energeia, Latinized as actus
· physical activity
· mental activity
· Activity
· Activity (UML)
· Activity, an alternative name for the game charades
· Activity, a task.
· Activity, the ability of a piece to influence the game in chess
· Activity, the rate of a catalytic reaction, such as enzyme activity, in physical chemistry and enzymology
· activity (chemistry), the effective concentration of a solute for the purposes of mass action
· activity (project management)
· activity (radioactivity), the number of radioactive decays per second
· activity (software engineering)
· activity (soil mechanics)
· activity diagram, a diagram representing activities in UML
· Activity, a board game by Piatnik
· HMS Activity, an aircraft carrier of the Royal Navy
· in military parlance, a military agency or unit (e.g. Intelligence Support Activity) .

Chapter 18. Food and Nutrition Services in Healthcare Facilities

Order	An order in a market such as a stock market, bond market or commodity market is an instruction from a customer to a broker to buy or sell on the exchange. These instructions can be simple or complicated. There are some standard instructions for such orders.
Hands	The Hands are the two intricate, prehensile, multi-fingered body parts normally located at the end of each arm of a primate. They are the chief organs for physically manipulating the environment, used for both gross motor skills and fine motor skills (such as picking up a small pebble). The fingertips contain some of the densest areas of nerve endings on the body, are the richest source of tactile feedback, and have the greatest positioning capability of the body; thus the sense of touch is intimately associated with Hands.
Personal	A personal ad is an item or notice traditionally in the newspaper, similar to a classified ad but personal in nature. In British English it is also commonly known as an advert in a lonely hearts column. With its rise in popularity, the World Wide Web has also become a common medium for personals, commonly referred to as online dating.
Technology	Technology is a broad concept that deals with human as well as other animal species` usage and knowledge of tools and crafts, and how it affects a species` ability to control and adapt to its environment. Technology is a term with origins in the Greek technología -- téchnÄ" (τî̃χνη), `craft` and -logía (-λογî̄ α), the study of something, or the branch of knowledge of a discipline. However, a strict definition is elusive; `Technology` can refer to material objects of use to humanity, such as machines, hardware or utensils, but can also encompass broader themes, including systems, methods of organization, and techniques.
Amenities	In the contexts of real estate and lodging, amenities are any tangible or intangible benefits of a property, especially those which increase the attractiveness or value of the property or which contribute to its comfort or convenience.
	Tangible amenities might include parks, swimming pools, health club facilities, party rooms, guest rooms (lodgings), theater or media rooms, bike paths, community centers, doormen, oyster bars or garages, for example.
	Intangible amenities might include a `pleasant view` or aspect, low crime rates, or a `sun-lit living room velu`, which all add to the living comforts of the property.
Digital	A digital system is a data technology that uses discrete (discontinuous) values. By contrast, non-digital (or analog) systems use a continuous range of values to represent information. Although digital representations are discrete, the information represented can be either discrete, such as numbers, letters or icons, or continuous, such as sounds, images, and other measurements of continuous systems.

209

Chapter 18. Food and Nutrition Services in Healthcare Facilities

Assessment	Educational Assessment is the process of documenting, usually in measurable terms, knowledge, skills, attitudes and beliefs. Assessment can focus on the individual learner, the learning community (class, workshop, or other organized group of learners), the institution, or the educational system as a whole. According to the Academic Exchange Quarterly: `Studies of a theoretical or empirical nature (including case studies, portfolio studies, exploratory, or experimental work) addressing the Assessment of learner aptitude and preparation, motivation and learning styles, learning outcomes in achievement and satisfaction in different educational contexts are all welcome, as are studies addressing issues of measurable standards and benchmarks`.
GROW model	The GROW model (or process) is a technique for problem solving or goal setting. It was developed in the UK and used extensively in the corporate coaching market in the late 1980s and 1990s. There have been many claims to authorship of GROW as a way of achieving goals and solving problems.
File sharing	File sharing is the practice of distributing or providing access to digitally stored information, such as computer programs, multi-media (audio, video), documents, transmission, and distribution models. Common methods are manual sharing using removable media, centralized computer file server installations on computer networks, World Wide Web-based hyperlinked documents, and the use of distributed peer-to-peer (P2P) networking.
Tray	A Tray is a shallow platform designed for carrying things. Famous Russian Zhostovo Tray. A seed Tray used in horticulture It is larger than a salver, a diminutive version commonly used for lighter and smaller servings, and it can be fashioned from numerous materials, including silver, brass, sheet iron, wood, melamine, and Papier-mâché. Some examples have raised galleries, handles, and short feet for support.
Revenue	Revenue is a crucial part of financial analysis. A company`s performance is measured to the extent to which its asset inflows (revenues) compare with its asset outflows (expenses). Net Income is the result of this equation, but revenue typically enjoys equal attention during a standard earnings call.
Choice	There are four types of decisions, although they can be expressed in different ways. Brian Tracy, who often uses enumerated lists in his talks, breaks them down into:

Chapter 18. Food and Nutrition Services in Healthcare Facilities

· Command decisions, which can only be made by you, as the `Commander in Chief`; or owner of a company.

· Delegated decisions, which may be made by anyone, such as the color of the bike shed, and should be delegated, as the decision must be made but the Choice is inconsequential.

· Avoided decisions, where the outcome could be so severe that the Choice should not be made, as the consequences can not be recovered from if the wrong Choice is made. This will most likely result in negative actions, such as death.

· `No-brainer` decisions, where the Choice is so obvious that only one Choice can reasonably be made.

A fifth type, however, or fourth if three and four are combined as one type, is the collaborative decision, which should be made in consultation with, and by agreement of others.

Hazard	A Hazard is usually used to describe a potentially harmful situation, although not usually the event itself; once the incident has started it is classified as an emergency or incident. There are many modes for a Hazard, which include: · Dormant - The situation has the potential to be Hazardous, but no people, property, or environment is currently affected by this. For instance, a hillside may be unstable, with the potential for a landslide, but there is nothing below or on the hillside that could be affected. · Potential - Also known as `Armed`, this is a situation wherein the Hazard is in the position to affect persons, property, or environment. This type of Hazard is likely to require further risk assessment. · Active - The Hazard is certain to cause harm, as no intervention is possible before the incident occurs. · Mitigated - A potential Hazard has been identified, but actions have been taken in order to ensure it does not become an incident.
Hazard analysis	A Hazard analysis is a process used to assess risk. The results of a Hazard analysis is the identification of unacceptable risks and the selection of means of controlling or eliminating them. The term is used in several engineering specialties, including avionics, chemical process safety, safety engineering and food safety.
Safety	Safety is the state of being `safe`, the condition of being protected against physical, social, spiritual, financial, political, emotional, occupational, psychological, educational or other types or consequences of failure, damage, error, accidents, harm or any other event which could be considered non-desirable. This can take the form of being protected from the event or from exposure to something that causes health or economical losses. It can include protection of people or of possessions.

Chapter 18. Food and Nutrition Services in Healthcare Facilities

Point	In typography, a point is the smallest unit of measure, being a subdivision of the larger pica. It is commonly abbreviated as pt. The traditional printer's point, from the era of hot metal typesetting and presswork, varied between 0.18 and 0.4 mm depending on various definitions of the foot.
	Today, the traditional point has been supplanted by the desktop publishing point (also called the PostScript point), which has been rounded to an even 72 points to the inch (1 point = $^{127}/_{360}$ mm ≈ 0.353 mm).
Maxima	In mathematics, maxima and minima, known collectively as extrema (singular: extremum), are the largest value (maximum) or smallest value (minimum), that a function takes in a point either within a given neighbourhood (local extremum) or on the function domain in its entirety (global extremum).
	Throughout, a Point refers to an input (x), while a value refers to an output (y): one distinguishing between the maximum value and the point (or points) at which it occurs.
	A real-valued function f defined on the real line is said to have a local (or relative) maximum point at the point x^*, if there exists some ε > 0, such that $f(x^*) \geq f(x)$ when $|x - x^*| < ε$.

Chapter 19. Business and Industry Foodservices

Business	A Business (, enterprise or firm) is a legally recognized organization designed to provide goods and/or services to consumers. Businesses are predominant in capitalist economies, most being privately owned and formed to earn profit that will increase the wealth of its owners and grow the Business itself. The owners and operators of a Business have as one of their main objectives the receipt or generation of a financial return in exchange for work and acceptance of risk.
Industry	An Industry is the manufacturing of a good or service within a category. Although Industry is a broad term for any kind of economic production, in economics and urban planning Industry is a synonym for the secondary sector, which is a type of economic activity involved in the manufacturing of raw materials into goods and products.
	There are four key industrial economic sectors: the primary sector, largely raw material extraction industries such as mining and farming; the secondary sector, involving refining, construction, and manufacturing; the tertiary sector, which deals with services and distribution of manufactured goods; and the quaternary sector, a relatively new type of knowledge Industry focusing on technological research, design and development such as computer programming, and biochemistry.
Call for bids	A Call for bids or call for tenders or invitation to tender (ITT) (often called tender for short) is a special procedure for generating competing offers from different bidders looking to obtain an award of business activity in works, supply).
	Open tenders, open calls for tenders, or advertised tenders are open to all vendors or contractors who can guarantee performance.
Contract	In common-law systems, the five key requirements for the creation of a Contract are: 1. offer and acceptance (agreement) 2. consideration 3. an intention to create legal relations 4. legal capacity 5. formalities
	In civil-law systems, the concept of consideration is not central. In addition, for some Contracts formalities must be complied with under what is sometimes called a statute of frauds.
	One of the most famous cases on forming a Contract is Carlill v. Carbolic Smoke Ball Company, decided in nineteenth-century England.
Contract management	Contract management or contract administration is the management of contracts made with customers, vendors, partners, or employees. Contract management includes negotiating the terms and conditions in contracts and ensuring compliance with the terms and conditions, as well as documenting and agreeing any changes that may arise during its implementation or execution. It can be summarized as the process of systematically and efficiently managing contract creating, execution, and analysis for the purpose of maximizing financial and operational performance and minimizing risk.

Chapter 19. Business and Industry Foodservices

Complexity	One of the problems in addressing Complexity issues has been distinguishing conceptually between the large number of variances in relationships extant in random collections, and the , but smaller, number of relationships between elements in systems where constraints (related to correlation of otherwise independent elements) simultaneously reduce the variations from element independence and create distinguishable regimes of more-uniform, relationships, or interactions. Weaver perceived and addressed this problem, in at least a preliminary way, in drawing a distinction between `disorganized Complexity` and `organized Complexity`. In Weaver`s view, disorganized Complexity results from the particular system having a very large number of parts, say millions of parts, or many more.
Commission	The Health and Safety Commission (HSC), was a United Kingdom non-departmental public body. The HSC was created by the Health and Safety at Work etc. Act 1974 (HSWA).
Rebate	A Rebate is an amount paid by way of reduction, return, or refund on what has already been paid or contributed. It is a type of sales promotion marketers use primarily as incentives or supplements to product sales. The mail-in Rebate is the most common.
Goal	A Goal or objective is a projected state of affairs that a person or a system plans or intends to achieve--a personal or organizational desired end-point in some sort of assumed development. Many people endeavor to reach Goals within a finite time by setting deadlines. A desire or an intention becomes a Goal if and only if one activates an action for achieving it .
Convenience	Convenience is anything that is intended to save resources (time, energy) or frustration. A Convenience store at a petrol station, for example, sells items that have nothing to do with gasoline/petrol, but it saves the consumer from having to go to a grocery store. `Convenience` is a very relative term and its meaning tends to change over time.
Convenience store	A Convenience store is a small store or shop that sells items such as candy, ice-cream, soft drinks, lottery tickets, newspapers and magazines, along with a selection of processed food and perhaps some groceries. Stores that are part of gas stations may also sell motor oil, windshield washer fluid, radiator fluid, and maps. Often toiletries and other hygiene products are stocked, and some of these stores also offer money orders and wire transfer services or liquor products.
Coffee	Coffee is an important necessity commodity. With over 501 billion cups consumed every year, Coffee is one of the world`s most popular beverages. Worldwide, 25 million small producers rely on Coffee for a living.
Organization	Management is interested in organization mainly from an instrumental point of view. For a company, organization is a means to an end to achieve its goals.

Chapter 19. Business and Industry Foodservices

Among the theories that are or have been most influential are:

· Pyramids or hierarchies
· Committees or juries
· Matrix organizations
· Ecologies

A hierarchy exemplifies an arrangement with a leader who leads leaders. This arrangement is often associated with bureaucracy.

Organizational chart	An organizational chart (often called organization chart, organigram(me))) is a diagram that shows the structure of an organization and the relationships and relative ranks of its parts and positions/jobs. The term is also used for similar diagrams, for example ones showing the different elements of a field of knowledge or a group of languages. The French Encyclopédie had one of the first organizational charts of knowledge in general.
Marketing	Marketing is a `social and managerial process by which individuals and groups obtain what they need and want through creating and exchanging products and values with others.` It is an integrated process through which companies create value for customers and build strong customer relationships in order to capture value from customers in return. marketing is used to create the customer, to keep the customer and to satisfy the customer. With the customer as the focus of its activities, it can be concluded that marketing management is one of the major components of business management.
Technology	Technology is a broad concept that deals with human as well as other animal species` usage and knowledge of tools and crafts, and how it affects a species` ability to control and adapt to its environment. Technology is a term with origins in the Greek technología -- téchnÄ" (τĨχνη), `craft` and -logía (-λογî¯ α), the study of something, or the branch of knowledge of a discipline. However, a strict definition is elusive; `Technology` can refer to material objects of use to humanity, such as machines, hardware or utensils, but can also encompass broader themes, including systems, methods of organization, and techniques.
Amenities	In the contexts of real estate and lodging, amenities are any tangible or intangible benefits of a property, especially those which increase the attractiveness or value of the property or which contribute to its comfort or convenience. Tangible amenities might include parks, swimming pools, health club facilities, party rooms, guest rooms (lodgings), theater or media rooms, bike paths, community centers, doormen, oyster bars or garages, for example.

Chapter 19. Business and Industry Foodservices

Intangible amenities might include a `pleasant view` or aspect, low crime rates, or a `sun-lit living room velu`, which all add to the living comforts of the property.

Chapter 20. Vending and Office Coffee Services

Cost	In business, retail, and accounting, a Cost is the value of money that has been used up to produce something, and hence is not available for use anymore. In economics, a Cost is an alternative that is given up as a result of a decision. In business, the Cost may be one of acquisition, in which case the amount of money expended to acquire it is counted as Cost.
Vending	A vending machine provides snacks, beverages, lottery tickets, and other products to consumers without a cashier. Items sold via these machines vary by country and region.
	In some countries, merchants may sell alcoholic beverages such as beer through vending machines, while other countries do not allow this practice (usually because of dram shop laws).
Coffee	Coffee is an important necessity commodity. With over 501 billion cups consumed every year, Coffee is one of the world`s most popular beverages. Worldwide, 25 million small producers rely on Coffee for a living.
Food and beverage	F'B is a common abbreviation in the United States and Commonwealth countries, including Hong Kong. F'B is typically the widely accepted abbreviation for `food and beverage,` which is the sector/industry that specializes in the conceptualization, the making of, and delivery of foods. The largest section of F'B employees are in restaurants and bars, including hotels, resorts, and casinos.
Co-creation	Co-creation is the practice of developing systems, products, companies and customers, or managers and employees. Isaac Newton said that in his great work, he stood on the shoulders of giants. Co-creation could be seen as creating great work by standing together with those for whom the project is intended.
Call for bids	A Call for bids or call for tenders or invitation to tender (ITT) (often called tender for short) is a special procedure for generating competing offers from different bidders looking to obtain an award of business activity in works, supply).
	Open tenders, open calls for tenders, or advertised tenders are open to all vendors or contractors who can guarantee performance.
Commission	The Health and Safety Commission (HSC), was a United Kingdom non-departmental public body. The HSC was created by the Health and Safety at Work etc. Act 1974 (HSWA).
Rebate	A Rebate is an amount paid by way of reduction, return, or refund on what has already been paid or contributed. It is a type of sales promotion marketers use primarily as incentives or supplements to product sales. The mail-in Rebate is the most common.
Automat	An Automat is a fast food restaurant where simple foods and drink are served by coin-operated and bill-operated vending machines.

Chapter 20. Vending and Office Coffee Services

Originally, the machines took only nickels but modern Automat vending machines accept bills. In the original format, a cashier would sit in a change booth in the center of the restaurant, behind a wide marble counter with five to eight rounded depressions in it.

Organization	Management is interested in organization mainly from an instrumental point of view. For a company, organization is a means to an end to achieve its goals. Among the theories that are or have been most influential are: · Pyramids or hierarchies · Committees or juries · Matrix organizations · Ecologies A hierarchy exemplifies an arrangement with a leader who leads leaders. This arrangement is often associated with bureaucracy.
Organizational chart	An organizational chart (often called organization chart, organigram(me))) is a diagram that shows the structure of an organization and the relationships and relative ranks of its parts and positions/jobs. The term is also used for similar diagrams, for example ones showing the different elements of a field of knowledge or a group of languages. The French Encyclopédie had one of the first organizational charts of knowledge in general.
Accounts payable	Accounts payable is a file or account that contains money that a person or company owes to suppliers, but has not paid yet (a form of debt). When you receive an invoice you add it to the file, and then you remove it when you pay. Thus, the A/P is a form of credit that suppliers offer to their purchasers by allowing them to pay for a product or service after it has already been received.
Accounts receivable	Accounts receivable (A/R) is one of a series of accounting transactions dealing with the billing of customers who owe money to a person, company or organization for goods and services that have been provided to the customer. In most business entities this is typically done by generating an invoice and mailing or electronically delivering it to the customer, who in turn must pay it within an established timeframe called credit or payment terms. An example of a common payment term is Net 30, which means payment is due in the amount of the invoice 30 days from the date of invoice.
Accountability	Accountability is a concept in ethics and governance with several meanings. It is often used synonymously with such concepts as responsibility, answerability, blameworthiness, liability, and other terms associated with the expectation of account-giving. As an aspect of governance, it has been central to discussions related to problems in the public sector, nonprofit and private (corporation) worlds.

227

Chapter 20. Vending and Office Coffee Services

Drop	A drop let is a small volume of liquid, bounded completely or almost completely by free surfaces. A drop may form when liquid accumulates at the lower end of a tube or other surface boundary, producing a hanging drop called a pendant drop. drops may also be formed by the condensation of a vapor or by atomization of a larger mass of liquid.
Marketing	Marketing is a `social and managerial process by which individuals and groups obtain what they need and want through creating and exchanging products and values with others.` It is an integrated process through which companies create value for customers and build strong customer relationships in order to capture value from customers in return. marketing is used to create the customer, to keep the customer and to satisfy the customer. With the customer as the focus of its activities, it can be concluded that marketing management is one of the major components of business management.
Sale	A sale is the pinnacle activity involved in selling products or services in return for money or other compensation. It is an act of completion of a commercial activity. A sale is completed by the seller, the owner of the goods.
Technology	Technology is a broad concept that deals with human as well as other animal species` usage and knowledge of tools and crafts, and how it affects a species` ability to control and adapt to its environment. Technology is a term with origins in the Greek technología -- téchnÄ" (τĨχνη), `craft` and -logía (-λογĨ α), the study of something, or the branch of knowledge of a discipline. However, a strict definition is elusive; `Technology` can refer to material objects of use to humanity, such as machines, hardware or utensils, but can also encompass broader themes, including systems, methods of organization, and techniques.
Amenities	In the contexts of real estate and lodging, amenities are any tangible or intangible benefits of a property, especially those which increase the attractiveness or value of the property or which contribute to its comfort or convenience. Tangible amenities might include parks, swimming pools, health club facilities, party rooms, guest rooms (lodgings), theater or media rooms, bike paths, community centers, doormen, oyster bars or garages, for example. Intangible amenities might include a `pleasant view` or aspect, low crime rates, or a `sun-lit living room velu`, which all add to the living comforts of the property.
Business	A Business (, enterprise or firm) is a legally recognized organization designed to provide goods and/or services to consumers. Businesses are predominant in capitalist economies, most being privately owned and formed to earn profit that will increase the wealth of its owners and grow the Business itself. The owners and operators of a Business have as one of their main objectives the receipt or generation of a financial return in exchange for work and acceptance of risk.

Chapter 20. Vending and Office Coffee Services

Industry	An Industry is the manufacturing of a good or service within a category. Although Industry is a broad term for any kind of economic production, in economics and urban planning Industry is a synonym for the secondary sector, which is a type of economic activity involved in the manufacturing of raw materials into goods and products.

There are four key industrial economic sectors: the primary sector, largely raw material extraction industries such as mining and farming; the secondary sector, involving refining, construction, and manufacturing; the tertiary sector, which deals with services and distribution of manufactured goods; and the quaternary sector, a relatively new type of knowledge Industry focusing on technological research, design and development such as computer programming, and biochemistry. |
| Services Marketing | Services marketing is marketing based on relationship and value. It may be used to market a service or a product.

Marketing a service-base business is different from marketing a goods-base business.

There are several major differences, including:

· The buyer purchases are intangible
· The service may be based on the reputation of a single person
· It`s more difficult to compare the quality of similar services
· The buyer cannot return the service

The major difference in the education of Services marketing versus regular marketing is that apart from the traditional `4 P`s,` Product, Price, Place, Promotion, there are three additional `P`s` consisting of People, Physical evidence, and Process. |
| Customer | A Customer buyer, is usually used to refer to a current or potential buyer or user of the products of an individual or organization, called the supplier, seller, or vendor. This is typically through purchasing or renting goods or services. However, in certain contexts, the term Customer also includes by extension anyone who uses or experiences the services of another. |
| Meeting | In a Meeting, two or more people come together for the purpose of discussing a (usually) predetermined topic such as business or community event planning, often in a formal setting.

In addition to coming together physically (in real life, face to face), communication lines and equipment can also be set up to have a discussion between people at different locations, e.g. a conference call or an e-Meeting.

In organizations, Meetings are an important vehicle for personal contact. |

231

Chapter 20. Vending and Office Coffee Services

Saleability	Saleability is a technical analysis term used to compare performances of different trading systems or different investments within one system. Note, it is not simply another word for profit. There are varying definitions for it, some as simple as the expected or average ratio of revenue to cost for a particular investment or trading system or `ratio of the number of winning trades or investments to the total number of trades or investments made, a number ranging from zero to 1.` Others can be complex or counter-intuitive.
Perpetual inventory	In business and accounting/accountancy, perpetual inventory or continuous inventory describes systems of inventory where information on inventory quantity and availability is updated on a continuous basis as a function of doing business. Generally this is accomplished by connecting the inventory system with order entry and in retail the point of sale system. In this case, book inventory would be exactly the same as, or almost the same, as the real inventory.
Micropayment	Micropayments are a means for transferring very small amounts of money, often in conjunction with the threshold pledge system, in situations where collecting such small amounts of money with the usual payment systems is impractical, in terms of the amount of money being collected. Early proposals for `Micropayments` were for transactions valued at as little as one thousandth of a US dollar, meaning a payment system that could efficiently handle payments at least as small as a mill, but now is often defined to mean payments too small to be affordably processed by credit card or other electronic transaction processing mechanism. The use of Micropayments may be called microcommerce.

232

Chapter 21. Private Club Management

Club	A Club is an association of two or more people united by a common interest or goal. A service Club, for example, exists for voluntary or charitable activities; there are Clubs devoted to hobbies and sports, social activities Clubs, political and religious Clubs, and so forth. Historically, Clubs occurred in all ancient states of which we have detailed knowledge.
Equity	Equity, in finance and accounting, is the residual claim or interest of the most junior class of investors in an asset, after all liabilities are paid. If valuations placed on assets do not exceed liabilities, negative Equity exists. In an accounting context, Shareholders` Equity (or stockholders` Equity, shareholders` funds, shareholders` capital or similar terms) represents the remaining interest in assets of a company, spread among individual shareholders of common or preferred stock.
Ownership	Ownership is the state or fact of exclusive rights and control over property, which may be an object, land/real estate or intellectual property. An ownership right is also referred to as title. The concept of ownership has existed for thousands of years and in all cultures.
Absolute advantage	In economics, Absolute advantage refers to the ability of a party (an individual, or country) to produce more of a good or service than competitors, using the same amount of resources. If a party has an Absolute advantage when using the same input as another party, it can produce a greater output. Since Absolute advantage is determined by a simple comparison of labor productivities, it is possible for a party to have no Absolute advantage in anything.
Tennis	Tennis is a sport played between two players (singles) or between two teams of two players each (doubles). Each player uses a strung racquet to strike a hollow rubber ball covered with felt over a net into the opponent`s court.  The modern game of Tennis originated in the United Kingdom in the late 19th century as `lawn Tennis` which has heavy connections to various field/lawn games as well as to the ancient game of real Tennis.
University	A university is an institution of higher education and research, which grants academic degrees in a variety of subjects. A university provides both undergraduate education and postgraduate education. The word university is derived from the Latin universitas magistrorum et scholarium, roughly meaning `community of teachers and scholars`.
Organization	Management is interested in organization mainly from an instrumental point of view. For a company, organization is a means to an end to achieve its goals. Among the theories that are or have been most influential are:

Chapter 21. Private Club Management

· Pyramids or hierarchies
· Committees or juries
· Matrix organizations
· Ecologies

A hierarchy exemplifies an arrangement with a leader who leads leaders. This arrangement is often associated with bureaucracy.

Restaurant	A restaurant prepares and serves food and drink to customers. Meals are generally served and eaten on premises, but many restaurant s also offer take-out and food delivery services. restaurant s vary greatly in appearance and offerings, including a wide variety of cuisines and service models.
The U.S.	The United States of America (commonly referred to as the United States, the U.S., the USA) is a federal constitutional republic comprising fifty states and a federal district. The country is situated mostly in central North America, where its forty-eight contiguous states and Washington, D.C., the capital district, lie between the Pacific and Atlantic Oceans, bordered by Canada to the north and Mexico to the south. The state of Alaska is in the northwest of the continent, with Canada to the east and Russia to the west across the Bering Strait.
Bylaw	Bylaw can refer to a law of local or limited application, passed under the authority of a higher law specifying what things may be regulated by the Bylaw, `Bylaw` is more frequently used in this context in Canada, the United Kingdom and some Commonwealth countries, whereas in the United States, the words code, ordinance or regulation are more frequent. Accordingly, a Bylaw enforcement officer is the Canadian equivalent of the American Code Enforcement Officer or Municipal Regulations Enforcement Officer.
Organizational chart	An organizational chart (often called organization chart, organigram(me))) is a diagram that shows the structure of an organization and the relationships and relative ranks of its parts and positions/jobs. The term is also used for similar diagrams, for example ones showing the different elements of a field of knowledge or a group of languages. The French Encyclopédie had one of the first organizational charts of knowledge in general.
Competency	Competence is the ability to perform a specific task, action or function successfully. Incompetence is its opposite. · Competence (biology), the ability of a cell to take up DNA · Competence (geology), the resistance of a rock against either erosion or deformation · Competence (human resources), a standardized requirement for an individual to properly perform a specific job · Competence (law), the mental capacity of an individual to participate in legal proceedings

237

Chapter 21. Private Club Management

· Competency evaluation (law)
· Jurisdiction, the authority of a legal body to deal with and make pronouncements on legal matters and, by implication, to administer justice within a defined area of responsibility
· Linguistic competence, the ability to speak and understand language.
· Communicative competence, the ability to speak and understand language. .

Food and beverage	F'B is a common abbreviation in the United States and Commonwealth countries, including Hong Kong. F'B is typically the widely accepted abbreviation for `food and beverage,` which is the sector/industry that specializes in the conceptualization, the making of, and delivery of foods. The largest section of F'B employees are in restaurants and bars, including hotels, resorts, and casinos.
Quality	Quality in business, engineering and manufacturing has a pragmatic interpretation as the non-inferiority or superiority of something. Quality is a perceptual, conditional and somewhat subjective attribute and may be understood differently by different people. Consumers may focus on the specification Quality of a product/service, or how it compares to competitors in the marketplace.
Call for bids	A Call for bids or call for tenders or invitation to tender (ITT) (often called tender for short) is a special procedure for generating competing offers from different bidders looking to obtain an award of business activity in works, supply). Open tenders, open calls for tenders, or advertised tenders are open to all vendors or contractors who can guarantee performance.
Competition	Co-operative Competition is based upon promoting mutual survival - `everyone wins`. Adam Smith`s `invisible hand` is a process where individuals compete to improve their level of happiness but compete in a cooperative manner through peaceful exchange and without violating other people. Cooperative Competition focuses individuals/groups/organisms against the environment.
Cost	In business, retail, and accounting, a Cost is the value of money that has been used up to produce something, and hence is not available for use anymore. In economics, a Cost is an alternative that is given up as a result of a decision. In business, the Cost may be one of acquisition, in which case the amount of money expended to acquire it is counted as Cost.
Technology	Technology is a broad concept that deals with human as well as other animal species` usage and knowledge of tools and crafts, and how it affects a species` ability to control and adapt to its environment. Technology is a term with origins in the Greek technología -- téchnÄ" (τῖχνη), `craft` and -logía (-λογῖ⁻ α), the study of something, or the branch of knowledge of a discipline. However, a strict definition is elusive; `Technology` can refer to material objects of use to humanity, such as machines, hardware or utensils, but can also encompass broader themes, including systems, methods of organization, and techniques.

Chapter 21. Private Club Management

Amenities	In the contexts of real estate and lodging, amenities are any tangible or intangible benefits of a property, especially those which increase the attractiveness or value of the property or which contribute to its comfort or convenience.
	Tangible amenities might include parks, swimming pools, health club facilities, party rooms, guest rooms (lodgings), theater or media rooms, bike paths, community centers, doormen, oyster bars or garages, for example.
	Intangible amenities might include a `pleasant view` or aspect, low crime rates, or a `sun-lit living room velu`, which all add to the living comforts of the property.
Resources	Human beings are also considered to be Resources because they have the ability to change raw materials into valuable Resources. The term Human Resources can also be defined as the skills, energies, talents, abilities and knowledge that are used for the production of goods or the rendering of services. While taking into account human beings as Resources, the following things have to be kept in mind:
	· The size of the population · The capabilities of the individuals in that population
	Many Resources cannot be consumed in their original form. They have to be processed in order to change them into more usable commodities.

Chapter 22. Cruise Lines: A Close Look at Resorts on Water

Popularity	Popularity is the quality of being well-liked or common. popularity figures are an important part of many people`s personal value systems, and forms a vital component of success in people-oriented fields such as Management, politics, Entertainment Industry among others.  Borrowed from the Latin popularis in 1490, originally meant common or `belonging to the people`.
Hotel manager	A Hotel manager or hotelier is a person who handles the everyday function and management of a hotel. Larger hotels often have management teams, instead of individual managers, where each member of the group begins to specialize on a certain area of interest. Some of the responsibilities of a Hotel manager include: · Organizing and directing the hotel`s services · Rooms · Front Office · Concierge · Reception · Reservations · Guest Service · Housekeeping · Floors · Laundry · Public Area · Catering · Entertainment · Engineering · Controlling budget and formulating financial plans · Financial · Promoting the business

243

· Marketing
· Sales
· Achieving profit and expense goals
· Meeting with customers, contractors and suppliers
· Hiring, training, reviewing and overseeing staff members

· Human Resource
· Attending to problems or customer complaints and comments
· Addressing maintenance and upkeep
· seeing to accommodations regular replacement and refurbishing

· furniture, carpet, linens
· meeting safety, health and licensing regulations

· Security

Background and Training of a Hotel manager

· Experience

· 3-5 years of experience in hotels at increasing levels of responsibility is desirable
· experience should include all phases, departments and shifts of hotel operation
· experience should include hotels in tourist areas as well as business hotels, specialized markets, etc.

· Training

· American Hotel and Lodging Association provides training courses recognized worldwide
· Training towards Certification in various hotel management departments is available through AHLA
· Certified Hotel Administrator (CHA) is one of the highest Certification through AHLA, indicating that a Hotel manager certified as a CHA is capable of running any hotel profitably and with high guest satisfaction

245

Chapter 22. Cruise Lines: A Close Look at Resorts on Water

Condominium	A Condominium, is the form of housing tenure and other real property where a specified part of a piece of real estate (usually of an apartment house) is individually owned while use of and access to common facilities in the piece such as hallways, heating system, elevators, exterior areas is executed under legal rights associated with the individual ownership and controlled by the association of owners that jointly represent ownership of the whole piece. Colloquially, the term is often used to refer to the unit itself in place of the word `apartment`. A Condominium may be simply defined as an `apartment` that the resident `owns` as opposed to rents.
Selling	Selling is trying to make sales by persuading someone to buy one's product or service. From a management viewpoint it is thought of as a part of marketing, although the skills required are different. Sales often forms a separate grouping in a corporate structure, employing separate specialist operatives known as salesmen (singular: salesman).
Travel agency	A travel agency is a retail business, that sells travel related products and services to customers, on behalf of suppliers, such as airlines, car rentals, cruise lines, hotels, railways, sightseeing tours and package holidays that combine several products. In addition to dealing with ordinary tourists, most travel agencies have a separate department devoted to making travel arrangements for business travelers and some travel agencies specialize in commercial and business travel only. There are also travel agencies that serve as general sales agents for foreign travel companies, allowing them to have offices in countries other than where their headquarters are located.
Yield	Yield is the compound rate of return that includes the effect of reinvesting interest or dividends.

Yield is the compound rate of return that includes the effect of reinvesting interest or dividends.

To the right is an example of a stock investment of one share purchased at the beginning of the year for $100.

· The quarterly dividend is reinvested at the quarter-end stock price.
· The number of shares purchased each quarter = ($ Dividend)/($ Stock Price).
· The final investment value of $103.02 is a 3.02% Yield on the initial investment of $100. This is the compound Yield, and this return can be considered to be the return on the investment of $100.

To calculate the rate of return, the investor includes the reinvested dividends in the total investment. The investor received a total of $4.06 in dividends over the year, all of which were reinvested, so the investment amount increased by $4.06.

· Total Investment = Cost Basis = $100 + $4.06 = $104.06.
· Capital gain/loss = $103.02 - $104.06 = -$1.04 (a capital loss)
· ($4.06 dividends - $1.04 capital loss) / $104.06 total investment = 2.9% ROI

Chapter 22. Cruise Lines: A Close Look at Resorts on Water

	The disadvantage of this ROI calculation is that it does not take into account the fact that not all the money was invested during the entire year (the dividend reinvestments occurred throughout the year).
Yield management	Yield management is the process of understanding, anticipating and influencing consumer behavior in order to maximize revenue or profits from a fixed, perishable resource This process was first discovered by Dr. Matt H. Keller. The challenge is to sell the right resources to the right customer at the right time for the right price. This process can result in price discrimination, where a firm charges customers consuming otherwise identical goods or services a different price for doing so.
Agent	Agent most commonly refers to:

· an entity that is capable of action, or `agency`
· one who acts for, or in the place of another, (the principal), by authority from him
· a title or honorific, such as `Agent Smith`

· Agent provocateur, person employed by the police or other entity to act undercover to entice or provoke another person to commit an illegal act
· Double Agent, counterintelligence term for someone who pretends to spy on a target organization on behalf of a controlling organization, but in fact is loyal to the target organization

· Triple Agent, pretends to be a double Agent for the target organization, but in fact is working for the controlling organization all along
· Special Agent, title for a detective or investigator for a state, county, municipal, federal or tribal government
· Secret Agent, spy involved in espionage

· Agent (law), in Commercial Law, is a person who is authorised to act on behalf of another (called the Principal) to create a legal relationship with a Third Party |

Chapter 22. Cruise Lines: A Close Look at Resorts on Water

· Election Agent, person legally responsible for the conduct of a candidate`s political campaign (UK)

· Free Agent, sports player whose contract with a team has expired

· Literary Agent, person who represents writers and their written works to publishers, theatrical producers and film producers

· Press Agent, professional publicist who acts on behalf of his or her client on all matters involving public relations

· Sports Agent, person who procures and negotiates employment and endorsement deals for a player

· Talent Agent or booking Agent, person who finds jobs for actors, musicians and models, etc., in various entertainment businesses

· Foreign Agent, person representing the interests of foreign powers, mandated by the Foreign Agents Registration Act to be identified to the American public

· Patent Agent or patent attorney, person who has the specialized qualifications necessary for representing clients in obtaining patents and acting in all matters and procedures relating to patent law and practice

· Real estate Agent or real estate broker, person who acts as an intermediary between sellers and buyers of real estate

· Travel Agent, person who works on behalf of a travel agency

· Tuition Agent, person who works on behalf of a tuition agency, specializing in introducing tutors to students requiring help in the academic area

· Yacht Agent or yacht broker, specialist who acts as a representative for the sale of a yacht or boat

· Agent , actor and decision maker in a model

· Homo economicus, concept in some economic theories of humans as rational and broadly self-interested actors

· Agent-Based Computational Economics, computational study of economic processes modeled as dynamic systems of interacting Agents

· Rational Agent, entity which has clear preferences, models uncertainty via expected values, and always chooses to perform the action that results in the optimal outcome for itself from among all feasible actions

· Representative Agent, refers to the typical decision-maker of a certain type

· A pharmacological Agent is a chemical substance with pharmacological or biological activity, i.e., a pharmaceutical drug

· Agent Orange, code name for an herbicide and defoliant
· Biological Agent, infectious disease or toxin that can be used in bioterrorism or biological warfare
· Chemical warfare, involves using the toxic properties of chemical substances as weapons to kill, injure, or incapacitate an enemy

· Blister Agent or vesicant, chemical compound that causes severe skin, eye and mucosal pain and irritation
· Blood Agent or cyanogen Agent, chemical compound carried by the blood for distribution throughout the body
· Incapacitating Agent, Agent that produces temporary physiological or mental effects, or both, which will render individuals incapable of concerted effort in the performance of their assigned duties
· Nerve Agent or nerve gases, class of phosphorus-containing organic chemicals (organophosphates) that disrupt the mechanism by which nerves transfer messages to organs
· Pulmonary Agent or choking Agent, chemical weapon Agent designed to impede a victim`s ability to breathe
· Riot control Agent, less-lethal lachrymatory Agents used for riot control

· Agent (grammar), the participant of a situation that carries out the action in this situation; also the name of the thematic role (also known as the thematic relation)
· Agent noun (or nomen Agentis), word that is derived from another word denoting an action, and that identifies an entity that does that action

· Agent architecture, blueprint for software Agents and intelligent control systems, depicting the arrangement of components
· Agent-based model, computational model for simulating the actions and interactions of autonomous individuals with a view to assessing their effects on the system as a whole
· Intelligent Agent, autonomous entity which observes and acts upon an environment and directs its activity towards achieving goals
· Software Agent, piece of software that acts for a user or other program in a relationship of agency

· Forté Agent, email and Usenet news client used on the Windows operating system
· User Agent, the client application used with a particular network protocol

Chapter 22. Cruise Lines: A Close Look at Resorts on Water

· Agent 47, fictional character and protagonist in the Hitman video-game series.
· Agent 212, name of a humorous Belgian comic about a large police officer
· Agent , group of characters in the series
· Agent (video game), currently in development by Rockstar North for the Playstation 3
· The Agent (film), 1922 film featuring Oliver Hardy
· Secret Agent (1936 film), British film directed by Alfred Hitchcock
· Agent, version of The Mole (TV series) that aired in Poland on TVN
· The Agents, superhuman characters in Seven Samurai 20XX
· Agents (band), a Finnish schlager/rock`n`roll band .

Revenue	Revenue is a crucial part of financial analysis. A company`s performance is measured to the extent to which its asset inflows (revenues) compare with its asset outflows (expenses). Net Income is the result of this equation, but revenue typically enjoys equal attention during a standard earnings call.
Competition	Co-operative Competition is based upon promoting mutual survival - `everyone wins`. Adam Smith`s `invisible hand` is a process where individuals compete to improve their level of happiness but compete in a cooperative manner through peaceful exchange and without violating other people. Cooperative Competition focuses individuals/groups/organisms against the environment.
Call for bids	A Call for bids or call for tenders or invitation to tender (ITT) (often called tender for short) is a special procedure for generating competing offers from different bidders looking to obtain an award of business activity in works, supply).
	Open tenders, open calls for tenders, or advertised tenders are open to all vendors or contractors who can guarantee performance.
Vacation	Most countries around the world have labor laws that mandate employers give a certain number of paid time-off days per year to workers. Nearly all Canadian provinces require at least two weeks, while in most of Europe the minimum is higher. US Where law does not mandate Vacation time, many employers nonetheless offer paid Vacation, typically 10 to 20 work days, to attract employees.
Industry	An Industry is the manufacturing of a good or service within a category. Although Industry is a broad term for any kind of economic production, in economics and urban planning Industry is a synonym for the secondary sector, which is a type of economic activity involved in the manufacturing of raw materials into goods and products.

255

Chapter 22. Cruise Lines: A Close Look at Resorts on Water

There are four key industrial economic sectors: the primary sector, largely raw material extraction industries such as mining and farming; the secondary sector, involving refining, construction, and manufacturing; the tertiary sector, which deals with services and distribution of manufactured goods; and the quaternary sector, a relatively new type of knowledge Industry focusing on technological research, design and development such as computer programming, and biochemistry.

Crimes

One can view criminalization as a procedure deployed by society as a pre-emptive, harm-reduction device, using the threat of punishment as a deterrent to anyone proposing to engage in the behavior causing harm. The State becomes involved because governing entities can become convinced that the costs of not criminalizing (i.e. allowing the harms to continue unabated) outweigh the costs of criminalizing it (restricting individual liberty, for example, in order to minimize harm to others).

Criminalization may provide future harm-reduction at least to the outside population, assuming those shamed or incarcerated or otherwise restrained for committing Crimes start out more prone to criminal behaviour.

Safety

Safety is the state of being `safe`, the condition of being protected against physical, social, spiritual, financial, political, emotional, occupational, psychological, educational or other types or consequences of failure, damage, error, accidents, harm or any other event which could be considered non-desirable. This can take the form of being protected from the event or from exposure to something that causes health or economical losses. It can include protection of people or of possessions.

Sea

A Sea generally refers to a large body of salt water, but the term is used in other contexts as well. Most commonly, the term refers to a large expanse of saline water connected with an ocean, and is commonly used as a synonym for ocean. It is also used sometimes to describe a large saline lake that lacks a natural outlet, such as the Caspian Sea.

)

· The Sea of Galilee is a small freshwater lake with a natural outlet, which is called Lake Tiberias or Lake Kinneret on modern Israeli maps, but its original name remains in use.
· The Sea of Cortés is more commonly known as the Gulf of California.
· The Persian Gulf is a Sea.
· The Dead Sea is actually a lake, as is the Caspian Sea and the mainly dried up Aral Sea.

Chapter 23. Casino Entertainment Management

Baccarat	Baccarat is a casino card game. It is believed to have been introduced into France from Italy during the reign of Charles VIII of France , and it is similar to Faro and to Basset. There are three accepted variants of the game: Baccarat chemin de fer, Baccarat banque (or à deux tableaux), and punto banco (or North American Baccarat).
Table	A table is both a mode of visual communication and a means of arranging data. The use of tables is pervasive throughout all communication, research and data analysis. Tables appear in print media, handwritten notes, computer software, architectural ornamentation, traffic signs and many other places.
Game	A Game is a structured activity, usually undertaken for enjoyment and , which is usually carried out for remuneration, and from art, which is more concerned with the expression of ideas. However, the distinction is not clear-cut, and many Games are also considered to be work (such as professional players of spectator sports/Games) or art (such as jigsaw puzzles or Games involving an artistic layout such as Mahjong solitaire).
Industry	An Industry is the manufacturing of a good or service within a category. Although Industry is a broad term for any kind of economic production, in economics and urban planning Industry is a synonym for the secondary sector, which is a type of economic activity involved in the manufacturing of raw materials into goods and products. There are four key industrial economic sectors: the primary sector, largely raw material extraction industries such as mining and farming; the secondary sector, involving refining, construction, and manufacturing; the tertiary sector, which deals with services and distribution of manufactured goods; and the quaternary sector, a relatively new type of knowledge Industry focusing on technological research, design and development such as computer programming, and biochemistry.
Dot.com bubble	The `Dot.com bubble` (or) was a speculative bubble covering roughly 1998-2001 (with a climax on March 10, 2000 with the NASDAQ peaking at 5132.52) during which stock markets in Western nations saw their equity value rise rapidly from growth in the more recent Internet sector and related fields. While the latter part was a boom and bust cycle, the Internet boom sometimes is meant to refer to the steady commercial growth of the Internet with the advent of the world wide web as exemplified by the first release of the Mosaic web browser in 1993 and continuing through the 1990s. The period was marked by the founding (and, in many cases, spectacular failure) of a group of new Internet-based companies commonly referred to as dot-coms.
Dog	· Canis familiaris · Canis familiaris domesticus

101

Chapter 23. Casino Entertainment Management

Go to **Cram101.com** for Interactive Practice Exams for this book or virtually any of your books for $4.95/month.
And, **NEVER** highlight a book again!

Chapter 23. Casino Entertainment Management

	The Dog is a domesticated form of the Gray Wolf, a member of the Canidae family of the order Carnivora. The term is used for both feral and pet varieties. The domestic Dog has been one of the most widely kept working and companion animals in human history.
Slot machine	A Slot machine (American), fruit machine (British)) is a casino gambling machine with three or more reels which spin when a button is pushed. Slots are also known as one-armed bandits because Slot machines were originally operated by a lever on the side of the machine (the one arm) instead of a button on the front panel, and because of their ability to leave the gamer penniless. Many modern machines still have a legacy lever in addition to the button.
Popularity	Popularity is the quality of being well-liked or common. popularity figures are an important part of many people's personal value systems, and forms a vital component of success in people-oriented fields such as Management, politics, Entertainment Industry among others. Borrowed from the Latin popularis in 1490, originally meant common or `belonging to the people`.
Stereotype	A stereotype is a commonly held public belief about specific social groups, based on some prior assumptions.
Amenities	In the contexts of real estate and lodging, amenities are any tangible or intangible benefits of a property, especially those which increase the attractiveness or value of the property or which contribute to its comfort or convenience. Tangible amenities might include parks, swimming pools, health club facilities, party rooms, guest rooms (lodgings), theater or media rooms, bike paths, community centers, doormen, oyster bars or garages, for example. Intangible amenities might include a `pleasant view` or aspect, low crime rates, or a `sun-lit living room velu`, which all add to the living comforts of the property.
Activities	Activity may mean:

· Action (philosophy), in general
· the Aristotelian concept of energeia, Latinized as actus
· physical activity
· mental activity
· Activity
· Activity (UML)
· Activity, an alternative name for the game charades
· Activity, a task.
· Activity, the ability of a piece to influence the game in chess
· Activity, the rate of a catalytic reaction, such as enzyme activity, in physical chemistry and enzymology
· activity (chemistry), the effective concentration of a solute for the purposes of mass action
· activity (project management)
· activity (radioactivity), the number of radioactive decays per second
· activity (software engineering)
· activity (soil mechanics)
· activity diagram, a diagram representing activities in UML
· Activity, a board game by Piatnik
· HMS Activity, an aircraft carrier of the Royal Navy
· in military parlance, a military agency or unit (e.g. Intelligence Support Activity) .

Organization	Management is interested in organization mainly from an instrumental point of view. For a company, organization is a means to an end to achieve its goals. Among the theories that are or have been most influential are: · Pyramids or hierarchies · Committees or juries · Matrix organizations · Ecologies A hierarchy exemplifies an arrangement with a leader who leads leaders. This arrangement is often associated with bureaucracy.
Organizational chart	An organizational chart (often called organization chart, organigram(me))) is a diagram that shows the structure of an organization and the relationships and relative ranks of its parts and positions/jobs. The term is also used for similar diagrams, for example ones showing the different elements of a field of knowledge or a group of languages. The French Encyclopédie had one of the first organizational charts of knowledge in general.

Chapter 23. Casino Entertainment Management

Revenue	Revenue is a crucial part of financial analysis. A company`s performance is measured to the extent to which its asset inflows (revenues) compare with its asset outflows (expenses). Net Income is the result of this equation, but revenue typically enjoys equal attention during a standard earnings call.
Security	Security is the degree of protection against danger, loss, and criminals.
	Security has to be compared and contrasted with other related concepts: Safety, continuity, reliability. The key difference between Security and reliability is that Security must take into account the actions of people attempting to cause destruction.
Collusion	Collusion is an agreement, usually secretive, which occurs between two or more persons to limit open competition by deceiving, misleading, or defrauding others of their legal rights or to obtain an objective forbidden by law typically by defrauding or gaining an unfair advantage. It is an agreement among firms to divide the market, set prices, or limit production. It can involve `wage fixing, kickbacks, or misrepresenting the independence of the relationship between the colluding parties.` All acts affected by Collusion are considered void.
Floating interest rate	A Floating interest rate, also known as a variable rate or adjustable rate, refers to any type of debt instrument, such as a loan, bond, mortgage, that does not have a fixed rate of interest over the life of the instrument.
	Such debt typically uses an index or other base rate for establishing the interest rate for each relevant period. One of the most common rates to use as the basis for applying interest rates is the London Inter-bank Offered Rate, or LIBOR (the rates at which large banks lend to each other).
Department	A Department is a part of a larger organization with a specific responsibility. For the division of organizations into Departments, see Departmentalization.
	In particular:
	· A government Department in Australia, Canada, Ireland, Sweden, Switzerland and the United States, corresponds to a ministry in other systems:
	· Department (Australian government) · Department (Swiss government) · Departments of the United Kingdom Government · Department (US government)

101

· Department (administrative division)- a geographical and administrative division within a country.
· Part of an institution such as a commercial company or a non-profit organization such as a university.

· Academic Department

· A Department store is a retail store that includes many specialized Departments such as clothing or household items.

· Part of a state or municipal government:

· Fire Department
· Police Department

· In the US military:

· `Department` is a term used by the U.S. Army, mostly prior to World War I.
· A naval Department is a section devoted to one of several major tasks.

· In the magazine context:

· Articles, essays and columns that follow a certain consistency under one topic. `

Technology

Technology is a broad concept that deals with human as well as other animal species` usage and knowledge of tools and crafts, and how it affects a species` ability to control and adapt to its environment. Technology is a term with origins in the Greek technología -- téchnÄ" (τĺχνη), `craft` and -logía (-λογĺ¯ α), the study of something, or the branch of knowledge of a discipline. However, a strict definition is elusive; `Technology` can refer to material objects of use to humanity, such as machines, hardware or utensils, but can also encompass broader themes, including systems, methods of organization, and techniques.

Chapter 23. Casino Entertainment Management

Chapter 23. Casino Entertainment Management

Drop	A drop let is a small volume of liquid, bounded completely or almost completely by free surfaces. A drop may form when liquid accumulates at the lower end of a tube or other surface boundary, producing a hanging drop called a pendant drop. drops may also be formed by the condensation of a vapor or by atomization of a larger mass of liquid.
Social	The term social refers to a characteristic of living organisms (humans in particular, though biologists also apply the term to populations of other animals). It always refers to the interaction of organisms with other organisms and to their collective co-existence, irrespective of whether they are aware of it or not, and irrespective of whether the interaction is voluntary or involuntary. In the absence of agreement about its meaning, the term `ps` is used in many different senses and regarded as a [[]], referringse among other things to: · Attitudes, orientations, or behaviours which take the interests, intentions, or needs of other people into account (in contrast to anti-social behaviour);has played some role in defining the idea or the principle. For instance terms like social realism, social justice, social constructivism, social psychology and social capital imply that there is some social process involved or considered, a process that is not there in regular, `non-social`, realism, justice, constructivism, psychology, or capital.
Crimes	One can view criminalization as a procedure deployed by society as a pre-emptive, harm-reduction device, using the threat of punishment as a deterrent to anyone proposing to engage in the behavior causing harm. The State becomes involved because governing entities can become convinced that the costs of not criminalizing (i.e. allowing the harms to continue unabated) outweigh the costs of criminalizing it (restricting individual liberty, for example, in order to minimize harm to others). Criminalization may provide future harm-reduction at least to the outside population, assuming those shamed or incarcerated or otherwise restrained for committing Crimes start out more prone to criminal behaviour.
Employee	Employment is a contract between two parties, one being the employer and the other being the employee. An employee may be defined as: `A person in the service of another under any contract of hire, express or implied, oral or written, where the employer has the power or right to control and direct the employee in the material details of how the work is to be performed.` Black`s Law Dictionary page 471 (5th ed. 1979). In a commercial setting, the employer conceives of a productive activity, generally with the intention of generating a profit, and the employee contributes labour to the enterprise, usually in return for payment of wages.

Chapter 23. Casino Entertainment Management

Employee assistance	Employee assistance Programs (EAPs) are employee benefit programs offered by many employers, typically in conjunction with a health insurance plan. EAPs are intended to help employees deal with personal problems that might adversely impact their work performance, health, and well-being. EAPs generally include assessment, short-term counseling and referral services for employees and their household members.
Employee assistance programs	Employee assistance programs (Employee assistance programss) are employee benefit programs offered by many employers, typically in conjunction with a health insurance plan. Employee assistance programss are intended to help employees deal with personal problems that might adversely impact their work performance, health, and well-being. Employee assistance programss generally include assessment, short-term counseling and referral services for employees and their household members.
Regulation	Regulation is `controlling human or societal behaviour by rules or restrictions.` Regulation can take many forms: legal restrictions promulgated by a government authority, self-Regulation, social Regulation (e.g. norms), co-Regulation and market Regulation. One can consider Regulation as actions of conduct imposing sanctions (such as a fine). This action of administrative law, or implementing regulatory law, may be contrasted with statutory or case law.
Regulations	The Control of Substances Hazardous to Health regulations 2002 is a United Kingdom Statutory Instrument that stipulates general requirements on employers to protect employees and other persons from the hazards of substances used at work by risk assessment, control of exposure, health surveillance and incident planning. There are also duties on employees to take care of their own exposure to hazardous substances and prohibitions on the import of certain substances into the European Economic Area. The regulations reenacted with amendements the Control of Substances Hazardous to Work regulations 1999 and implement several European Union directives.
Program	The Program (or Project) Evaluation and Review Technique, commonly abbreviated PERT, is a model for project management designed to analyze and represent the tasks involved in completing a given project.
	PERT is a method to analyze the involved tasks in completing a given project, especially the time needed to complete each task, and identifying the minimum time needed to complete the total project.
	PERT was developed primarily to simplify the planning and scheduling of large and complex projects.
Resources	Human beings are also considered to be Resources because they have the ability to change raw materials into valuable Resources. The term Human Resources can also be defined as the skills, energies, talents, abilities and knowledge that are used for the production of goods or the rendering of services. While taking into account human beings as Resources, the following things have to be kept in mind:

271

Chapter 23. Casino Entertainment Management

· The size of the population
· The capabilities of the individuals in that population

Many Resources cannot be consumed in their original form. They have to be processed in order to change them into more usable commodities.

Competition	Co-operative Competition is based upon promoting mutual survival - `everyone wins`. Adam Smith`s `invisible hand` is a process where individuals compete to improve their level of happiness but compete in a cooperative manner through peaceful exchange and without violating other people. Cooperative Competition focuses individuals/groups/organisms against the environment.
Globalization	Globalization (or globalisation) describes an ongoing process by which regional economies, societies, and cultures have become integrated through a globe-spanning network of communication and exchange. The term is sometimes used to refer specifically to economic Globalization: the integration of national economies into the international economy through trade, foreign direct investment, capital flows, migration, and the spread of technology. However, Globalization is usually recognized as being driven by a combination of economic, technological, sociocultural, political, and biological factors.
Adaptability	Adaptability (lat.: adaptÅ = fit, matching) is a feature of a system or of a process. This word has been put to use as a specialised term in different disciplines and in business operations. Word definitions of Adaptability as a specialised term differ little from dictionary definitions.

Chapter 24. Sports and Recreational Foodservices: Part of the Leisure Service Market

Industry	An Industry is the manufacturing of a good or service within a category. Although Industry is a broad term for any kind of economic production, in economics and urban planning Industry is a synonym for the secondary sector, which is a type of economic activity involved in the manufacturing of raw materials into goods and products.
	There are four key industrial economic sectors: the primary sector, largely raw material extraction industries such as mining and farming; the secondary sector, involving refining, construction, and manufacturing; the tertiary sector, which deals with services and distribution of manufactured goods; and the quaternary sector, a relatively new type of knowledge Industry focusing on technological research, design and development such as computer programming, and biochemistry.
Time	Time is a component of the measuring system used to sequence events, to compare the durations of events and the intervals between them, and to quantify the motions of objects. Time has been a major subject of religion, philosophy, and science, but defining it in a non-controversial manner applicable to all fields of study has consistently eluded the greatest scholars.
	In physics and other sciences, Time is considered one of the few fundamental quantities.
Organizational structure	An Organizational structure is a mainly hierarchical concept of subordination of entities that collaborate and contribute to serve one common aim.
	Organizations are a variant of clustered entities. An organization can be structured in many different ways and styles, depending on their objectives and ambiance.
Organization	Management is interested in organization mainly from an instrumental point of view. For a company, organization is a means to an end to achieve its goals.
	Among the theories that are or have been most influential are:
	· Pyramids or hierarchies · Committees or juries · Matrix organizations · Ecologies
	A hierarchy exemplifies an arrangement with a leader who leads leaders. This arrangement is often associated with bureaucracy.

275

Chapter 24. Sports and Recreational Foodservices: Part of the Leisure Service Market

Organizational chart	An organizational chart (often called organization chart, organigram(me))) is a diagram that shows the structure of an organization and the relationships and relative ranks of its parts and positions/jobs. The term is also used for similar diagrams, for example ones showing the different elements of a field of knowledge or a group of languages. The French Encyclopédie had one of the first organizational charts of knowledge in general.
Vending	A vending machine provides snacks, beverages, lottery tickets, and other products to consumers without a cashier. Items sold via these machines vary by country and region. In some countries, merchants may sell alcoholic beverages such as beer through vending machines, while other countries do not allow this practice (usually because of dram shop laws).
Activities	Activity may mean: · Action (philosophy), in general · the Aristotelian concept of energeia, Latinized as actus · physical activity · mental activity · Activity · Activity (UML) · Activity, an alternative name for the game charades · Activity, a task. · Activity, the ability of a piece to influence the game in chess · Activity, the rate of a catalytic reaction, such as enzyme activity, in physical chemistry and enzymology · activity (chemistry), the effective concentration of a solute for the purposes of mass action · activity (project management) · activity (radioactivity), the number of radioactive decays per second · activity (software engineering) · activity (soil mechanics) · activity diagram, a diagram representing activities in UML · Activity, a board game by Piatnik · HMS Activity, an aircraft carrier of the Royal Navy · in military parlance, a military agency or unit (e.g. Intelligence Support Activity) .
Revenue	Revenue is a crucial part of financial analysis. A company's performance is measured to the extent to which its asset inflows (revenues) compare with its asset outflows (expenses). Net Income is the result of this equation, but revenue typically enjoys equal attention during a standard earnings call.
Accounting	Accountancy is the art of communicating financial information about a business entity to users such as shareholders and managers. The communication is generally in the form of financial statements that show in money terms the economic resources under the control of management.

nonsense

TCM = TR – TVC

The Unit Contribution margin (C) is Unit Revenue (Price, P) minus Unit Variable Cost (V):

C = P – V

The Contribution margin Ratio is the percentage of Contribution over Total Revenue, which can be calculated from the unit contribution over unit price or total contribution over Total Revenue:

$$\frac{C}{P} = \frac{P-V}{P} = \frac{\text{Unit Contribution Margin}}{\text{Price}} = \frac{\text{Total Contribution Margin}}{\text{Total Revenue}}$$

For instance, if the price is $10 and the unit variable cost is $2, then the unit Contribution margin is $8, and the Contribution margin ratio is $8/$10 = 80%.

Pricing	Pricing is a fundamental aspect of financial modelling, and is one of the four Ps of the marketing mix. The other three aspects are product, promotion, and place. It is also a key variable in microeconomic price allocation theory.
Sale	A sale is the pinnacle activity involved in selling products or services in return for money or other compensation. It is an act of completion of a commercial activity. A sale is completed by the seller, the owner of the goods.
Anecdotal value	In economics, Anecdotal value refers to the primarily social and political value of an anecdote or anecdotal evidence in promoting understanding of a social, cultural, in the last several decades the evaluation of anecdotes has received sustained academic scrutiny from economists and scholars such as S.G. Checkland (on David Ricardo), Steven Novella, Hollis Robbins, R. Charleton, Kwamena Kwansah-Aidoo, and others; these academics seek to quantify the value inherent in the deployment of anecdotes. More recently, economists studying choice models have begun assessing Anecdotal value in the context of framing; Kahneman and Tversky suggest that choice models may be contingent on stories or anecdotes that frame or influence choice.
Recession	In economics, a Recession is a general slowdown in economic activity over a sustained period of time, or a business cycle contraction. During Recession s, many macroeconomic indicators vary in a similar way. Production as measured by Gross Domestic Product (GDP), employment, investment spending, capacity utilization, household incomes and business profits all fall during Recession s.

281

Chapter 24. Sports and Recreational Foodservices: Part of the Leisure Service Market

Business	A Business (, enterprise or firm) is a legally recognized organization designed to provide goods and/or services to consumers. Businesses are predominant in capitalist economies, most being privately owned and formed to earn profit that will increase the wealth of its owners and grow the Business itself. The owners and operators of a Business have as one of their main objectives the receipt or generation of a financial return in exchange for work and acceptance of risk.
Saleability	Saleability is a technical analysis term used to compare performances of different trading systems or different investments within one system. Note, it is not simply another word for profit. There are varying definitions for it, some as simple as the expected or average ratio of revenue to cost for a particular investment or trading system or `ratio of the number of winning trades or investments to the total number of trades or investments made, a number ranging from zero to 1.` Others can be complex or counter-intuitive.
Technology	Technology is a broad concept that deals with human as well as other animal species` usage and knowledge of tools and crafts, and how it affects a species` ability to control and adapt to its environment. Technology is a term with origins in the Greek technología -- téchnÄ" (τῖχνη), `craft` and -logía (-λογῖ α), the study of something, or the branch of knowledge of a discipline. However, a strict definition is elusive; `Technology` can refer to material objects of use to humanity, such as machines, hardware or utensils, but can also encompass broader themes, including systems, methods of organization, and techniques.
Value	A personal and cultural value is a relative ethic value, an assumption upon which implementation can be extrapolated. A value system is a set of consistent values and measures that are not true. A principle value is a foundation upon which other values and measures of integrity are based.
Amenities	In the contexts of real estate and lodging, amenities are any tangible or intangible benefits of a property, especially those which increase the attractiveness or value of the property or which contribute to its comfort or convenience. Tangible amenities might include parks, swimming pools, health club facilities, party rooms, guest rooms (lodgings), theater or media rooms, bike paths, community centers, doormen, oyster bars or garages, for example. Intangible amenities might include a `pleasant view` or aspect, low crime rates, or a `sun-lit living room velu`, which all add to the living comforts of the property.

Chapter 25. Management of Amusement and Theme Parks

Industry	An Industry is the manufacturing of a good or service within a category. Although Industry is a broad term for any kind of economic production, in economics and urban planning Industry is a synonym for the secondary sector, which is a type of economic activity involved in the manufacturing of raw materials into goods and products. There are four key industrial economic sectors: the primary sector, largely raw material extraction industries such as mining and farming; the secondary sector, involving refining, construction, and manufacturing; the tertiary sector, which deals with services and distribution of manufactured goods; and the quaternary sector, a relatively new type of knowledge Industry focusing on technological research, design and development such as computer programming, and biochemistry.
Time	Time is a component of the measuring system used to sequence events, to compare the durations of events and the intervals between them, and to quantify the motions of objects. Time has been a major subject of religion, philosophy, and science, but defining it in a non-controversial manner applicable to all fields of study has consistently eluded the greatest scholars. In physics and other sciences, Time is considered one of the few fundamental quantities.
Walt Disney	Walter Elias `Walt` Disney (December 5, 1901 - December 15, 1966) was an American film producer, director, screenwriter, voice actor, animator, entrepreneur, entertainer, international icon and philanthropist. Disney is famous for his influence in the field of entertainment during the twentieth century. As the co-founder (with his brother Roy O. Disney) of Walt Disney Productions, Disney became one of the best-known motion picture producers in the world.
Competition	Co-operative Competition is based upon promoting mutual survival - `everyone wins`. Adam Smith`s `invisible hand` is a process where individuals compete to improve their level of happiness but compete in a cooperative manner through peaceful exchange and without violating other people. Cooperative Competition focuses individuals/groups/organisms against the environment.
Multiplier effect	In economics, the multiplier effect or spending multiplier is the idea that an initial amount of spending (usually by the government) leads to increased consumption spending and so results in an increase in national income greater than the initial amount of spending. In other words, an initial change in aggregate demand causes a change in aggregate output for the economy that is a multiple of the initial change. However, multiplier values less than one have been empirical measured, suggesting that government spending crowds out private investments and spending that would have otherwise happened.

Chapter 25. Management of Amusement and Theme Parks

Anecdotal value	In economics, Anecdotal value refers to the primarily social and political value of an anecdote or anecdotal evidence in promoting understanding of a social, cultural, in the last several decades the evaluation of anecdotes has received sustained academic scrutiny from economists and scholars such as S.G. Checkland (on David Ricardo), Steven Novella, Hollis Robbins, R. Charleton, Kwamena Kwansah-Aidoo, and others; these academics seek to quantify the value inherent in the deployment of anecdotes. More recently, economists studying choice models have begun assessing Anecdotal value in the context of framing; Kahneman and Tversky suggest that choice models may be contingent on stories or anecdotes that frame or influence choice.
Saleability	Saleability is a technical analysis term used to compare performances of different trading systems or different investments within one system. Note, it is not simply another word for profit. There are varying definitions for it, some as simple as the expected or average ratio of revenue to cost for a particular investment or trading system or `ratio of the number of winning trades or investments to the total number of trades or investments made, a number ranging from zero to 1.` Others can be complex or counter-intuitive.
Business	A Business (, enterprise or firm) is a legally recognized organization designed to provide goods and/or services to consumers. Businesses are predominant in capitalist economies, most being privately owned and formed to earn profit that will increase the wealth of its owners and grow the Business itself. The owners and operators of a Business have as one of their main objectives the receipt or generation of a financial return in exchange for work and acceptance of risk.
Kiosk	In the Mediterranean Basin and the Near East, a Kiosk is a small, separated garden pavilion open on some or all sides. Kiosks were common in Persia, India, Pakistan, and in the Ottoman Empire from the 13th century onward. Today, there are many Kiosks in and around the Topkapı Palace in Istanbul, and they are still a relatively common sight in Greece.
Technology	Technology is a broad concept that deals with human as well as other animal species` usage and knowledge of tools and crafts, and how it affects a species` ability to control and adapt to its environment. Technology is a term with origins in the Greek technología -- téchnÄ" (τῐ̀χνη), `craft` and -logía (-λογῐ̄ α), the study of something, or the branch of knowledge of a discipline. However, a strict definition is elusive; `Technology` can refer to material objects of use to humanity, such as machines, hardware or utensils, but can also encompass broader themes, including systems, methods of organization, and techniques.
Virtual	The term virtual is a concept applied in many fields with somewhat differing connotations, and also, differing denotations. The term has been defined in philosophy as `that which is not real` but may display the salient qualities of the real. Colloquially, virtual is used to mean almost, particularly when used in the adverbial form e.g., `That`s virtual ly [almost] impossible`.

Chapter 25. Management of Amusement and Theme Parks

Virtual queuing	Virtual queuing is a concept used in inbound call centers. Call centers use an Automatic Call Distributor (ACD) to distribute incoming calls to specific resources (agents) in the center. ACDs hold queued calls in First In, First Out order until agents become available.
Amenities	In the contexts of real estate and lodging, amenities are any tangible or intangible benefits of a property, especially those which increase the attractiveness or value of the property or which contribute to its comfort or convenience. Tangible amenities might include parks, swimming pools, health club facilities, party rooms, guest rooms (lodgings), theater or media rooms, bike paths, community centers, doormen, oyster bars or garages, for example. Intangible amenities might include a `pleasant view` or aspect, low crime rates, or a `sun-lit living room velu`, which all add to the living comforts of the property.
Restaurant	A restaurant prepares and serves food and drink to customers. Meals are generally served and eaten on premises, but many restaurant s also offer take-out and food delivery services. restaurant s vary greatly in appearance and offerings, including a wide variety of cuisines and service models.
Americans with Disabilities Act	The Americans with Disabilities Act of 1990 (ADA) is the short title of United States (Pub.L. 101-336, 104 Stat. 327, enacted July 26, 1990), codified at 42 U.S.C. § 12101 et seq. It was signed into law on July 26, 1990, by President George H. W. Bush, and later amended with changes effective January 1, 2009. The ADA is a wide-ranging civil rights law that prohibits, under certain circumstances, discrimination based on disability. It affords similar protections against discrimination to Americans with disabilities as the Civil Rights Act of 1964, which made discrimination based on race, religion, sex, national origin, and other characteristics illegal.
Safety	Safety is the state of being `safe`, the condition of being protected against physical, social, spiritual, financial, political, emotional, occupational, psychological, educational or other types or consequences of failure, damage, error, accidents, harm or any other event which could be considered non-desirable. This can take the form of being protected from the event or from exposure to something that causes health or economical losses. It can include protection of people or of possessions.
Security	Security is the degree of protection against danger, loss, and criminals. Security has to be compared and contrasted with other related concepts: Safety, continuity, reliability. The key difference between Security and reliability is that Security must take into account the actions of people attempting to cause destruction.
Risk	Risk concerns the expected value of one or more results of one or more future events. Technically, the value of those results may be positive or negative. However, general usage tends focus only on potential harm that may arise from a future event, which may accrue either from incurring a cost (`downside Risk`) or by failing to attain some benefit (`upside Risk`).

101

Chapter 25. Management of Amusement and Theme Parks

Chapter 25. Management of Amusement and Theme Parks

Risk management	Example of Risk management: NASA`s illustration showing high impact risk areas for the International Space Station`. Risk management is the identification, assessment, and prioritization of risks followed by coordinated and economical application of resources to minimize, monitor, and control the probability and/or impact of unfortunate events. Risks can come from uncertainty in financial markets, project failures, legal liabilities, credit risk, accidents, natural causes and disasters as well as deliberate attacks from an adversary. Several Risk management standards have been developed including the Project Management Institute, the National Institute of Science and Technology, actuarial societies, and ISO standards.
Career	Career is a term defined by the Oxford English Dictionary as an individual`s `course or progress through life `. It is usually considered to pertain to remunerative work (and sometimes also formal education). The etymology of the term is somewhat ironic in that it comes from the Latin word carrera, which means race .
Organization	Management is interested in organization mainly from an instrumental point of view. For a company, organization is a means to an end to achieve its goals. Among the theories that are or have been most influential are: · Pyramids or hierarchies · Committees or juries · Matrix organizations · Ecologies A hierarchy exemplifies an arrangement with a leader who leads leaders. This arrangement is often associated with bureaucracy.
Organizational chart	An organizational chart (often called organization chart, organigram(me))) is a diagram that shows the structure of an organization and the relationships and relative ranks of its parts and positions/jobs. The term is also used for similar diagrams, for example ones showing the different elements of a field of knowledge or a group of languages. The French Encyclopédie had one of the first organizational charts of knowledge in general.
Department	A Department is a part of a larger organization with a specific responsibility. For the division of organizations into Departments, see Departmentalization. In particular:

Chapter 25. Management of Amusement and Theme Parks

· A government Department in Australia, Canada, Ireland, Sweden, Switzerland and the United States, corresponds to a ministry in other systems:

· Department (Australian government)
· Department (Swiss government)
· Departments of the United Kingdom Government
· Department (US government)

· Department (administrative division)- a geographical and administrative division within a country.
· Part of an institution such as a commercial company or a non-profit organization such as a university.

· Academic Department

· A Department store is a retail store that includes many specialized Departments such as clothing or household items.

· Part of a state or municipal government:

· Fire Department
· Police Department

· In the US military:

· `Department` is a term used by the U.S. Army, mostly prior to World War I.
· A naval Department is a section devoted to one of several major tasks.

· In the magazine context:

· Articles, essays and columns that follow a certain consistency under one topic. `

Employment

Employment is a contract between two parties, one being the employer and the other being the employee. An employee may be defined as: `A person in the service of another under any contract of hire, express or implied, oral or written, where the employer has the power or right to control and direct the employee in the material details of how the work is to be performed.` Black`s Law Dictionary page 471 (5th ed. 1979).

In a commercial setting, the employer conceives of a productive activity, generally with the intention of generating a profit, and the employee contributes labour to the enterprise, usually in return for payment of wages.

Opportunities

`opportunities (Let`s Make Lots of Money)` is a song by UK synthpop duo Pet Shop Boys, released as a single in 1985 and then in 1986, gaining greater popularity in both the UK and U.S. with its second release.

Written as a satire of Thatcherism and its embodiment in conspicuous consumption and yuppies in the United Kingdom during the 1980s, the song`s indirect attack on its subject matter has come to exemplify the Pet Shop Boys as ironists in their songwriting.

The song was written during the Pet Shop Boys` formative years, in 1983. According to Neil Tennant, the main lyrical concept came while in a recording studio in Camden Town when Chris Lowe asked him to make up a lyric based around the line `Let`s make lots of money`.

Accounts payable

Accounts payable is a file or account that contains money that a person or company owes to suppliers, but has not paid yet (a form of debt). When you receive an invoice you add it to the file, and then you remove it when you pay. Thus, the A/P is a form of credit that suppliers offer to their purchasers by allowing them to pay for a product or service after it has already been received.

Accounts receivable

Accounts receivable (A/R) is one of a series of accounting transactions dealing with the billing of customers who owe money to a person, company or organization for goods and services that have been provided to the customer. In most business entities this is typically done by generating an invoice and mailing or electronically delivering it to the customer, who in turn must pay it within an established timeframe called credit or payment terms.

An example of a common payment term is Net 30, which means payment is due in the amount of the invoice 30 days from the date of invoice.

Cost

In business, retail, and accounting, a Cost is the value of money that has been used up to produce something, and hence is not available for use anymore. In economics, a Cost is an alternative that is given up as a result of a decision. In business, the Cost may be one of acquisition, in which case the amount of money expended to acquire it is counted as Cost.

Go to **Cram101.com** for Interactive Practice Exams for this book or virtually any of your books for $4.95/month.
And, **NEVER** highlight a book again!

Chapter 26. Overview of the Entertainment Industry

Industry	An Industry is the manufacturing of a good or service within a category. Although Industry is a broad term for any kind of economic production, in economics and urban planning Industry is a synonym for the secondary sector, which is a type of economic activity involved in the manufacturing of raw materials into goods and products. There are four key industrial economic sectors: the primary sector, largely raw material extraction industries such as mining and farming; the secondary sector, involving refining, construction, and manufacturing; the tertiary sector, which deals with services and distribution of manufactured goods; and the quaternary sector, a relatively new type of knowledge Industry focusing on technological research, design and development such as computer programming, and biochemistry.
Product	When a product reaches the maturity stage of the product life cycle a company may choose to operate strategies to extend the life of the product. If the product is predicted to continue to be successful or an upgrade is soon to be released the company can use various methods to keep sales, else the product will be left as is to continue to the decline stage. Examples of extension strategies are: · Discounted price · Increased advertising · Accessing another market abroad Another strategy is added value. This is a widely used extension strategy.
Infotainment	Infotainment is `information-based media content or programming that also includes entertainment content in an effort to enhance popularity with audiences and consumers.` It is a neologistic portmanteau of information and entertainment, referring to a type of media which provides a combination of information and entertainment. According to many dictionaries infotainment is always television, and the term is `mainly disapproving.` However, many self-described infotainment websites exist, which provide a variety of functions and services. The label `infotainment` is emblematic of concern and criticism that journalism is devolving from a medium which conveys serious information about issues that affect the public interest, into a form of entertainment which happens to have fresh `facts` in the mix.

Chapter 26. Overview of the Entertainment Industry

Chapter 26. Overview of the Entertainment Industry

Multiple comparisons	In statistics, the multiple comparisons (or `multiple testing`) problem occurs when one considers a set, of statistical inferences simultaneously. Errors in inference, including confidence intervals that fail to include their corresponding population parameters, or hypothesis tests that incorrectly reject the null hypothesis, are more likely to occur when one considers the family as a whole. Several statistical techniques have been developed to prevent this from happening, allowing significance levels for single and multiple comparisons to be directly compared.
Dot.com bubble	The `Dot.com bubble` (or) was a speculative bubble covering roughly 1998-2001 (with a climax on March 10, 2000 with the NASDAQ peaking at 5132.52) during which stock markets in Western nations saw their equity value rise rapidly from growth in the more recent Internet sector and related fields. While the latter part was a boom and bust cycle, the Internet boom sometimes is meant to refer to the steady commercial growth of the Internet with the advent of the world wide web as exemplified by the first release of the Mosaic web browser in 1993 and continuing through the 1990s. The period was marked by the founding (and, in many cases, spectacular failure) of a group of new Internet-based companies commonly referred to as dot-coms.
Trend	A trend is a line of general direction of movement, a prevailing tendency of inclination, a style or preference, a line of development, `trend` is a synonym to `tendency`. A fad is a practice or interest followed for a time with exaggerated zeal.
Business	A Business (, enterprise or firm) is a legally recognized organization designed to provide goods and/or services to consumers. Businesses are predominant in capitalist economies, most being privately owned and formed to earn profit that will increase the wealth of its owners and grow the Business itself. The owners and operators of a Business have as one of their main objectives the receipt or generation of a financial return in exchange for work and acceptance of risk.
Career	Career is a term defined by the Oxford English Dictionary as an individual's `course or progress through life `. It is usually considered to pertain to remunerative work (and sometimes also formal education). The etymology of the term is somewhat ironic in that it comes from the Latin word carrera, which means race .
Collective	A commune or intentional community, which may also be known as a `collective household`, is a group of people who live together in some kind of dwelling or residence, or in some other arrangement (eg. sharing land). collective households may be organized for a specific purpose .

299

Chapter 26. Overview of the Entertainment Industry

Collective bargaining	In organized labor, Collective bargaining is the method whereby workers organize together (usually in unions) to meet, converse, and negotiate upon the work conditions with their employers normally resulting in a written contract setting forth the wages, hours, and other conditions to be observed for a stipulated period. It is the practice in which union and company representatives meet to negotiate a new labor contract. In various national labor and employment law contexts, the term Collective bargaining takes on a more specific legal meaning.
Production manager	Theatrical production management is a sub-division of stagecraft. The production management team (consisting of a production manager and any number of assistants) is responsible for realizing the visions of the producer and the director or choreographer within constraints of technical possibility. This involves coordinating the operations of various production sub-disciplines (scenic, wardrobe, lighting, sound, projection, automation, video, pyrotechnics, stage management, etc).
Public relations	Public relations is the practice of managing the communication between an organization and its publics. Public relations gains an organization or individual exposure to their audiences using topics of public interest and news items that do not require direct payment. Because Public relations places exposure in credible third-party outlets, it offers a third-party legitimacy that advertising does not have.
Agent	Agent most commonly refers to: · an entity that is capable of action, or `agency` · one who acts for, or in the place of another, (the principal), by authority from him · a title or honorific, such as `Agent Smith` · Agent provocateur, person employed by the police or other entity to act undercover to entice or provoke another person to commit an illegal act · Double Agent, counterintelligence term for someone who pretends to spy on a target organization on behalf of a controlling organization, but in fact is loyal to the target organization · Triple Agent, pretends to be a double Agent for the target organization, but in fact is working for the controlling organization all along · Special Agent, title for a detective or investigator for a state, county, municipal, federal or tribal government · Secret Agent, spy involved in espionage · Agent (law), in Commercial Law, is a person who is authorised to act on behalf of another (called the Principal) to create a legal relationship with a Third Party

· Election Agent, person legally responsible for the conduct of a candidate`s political campaign (UK)

· Free Agent, sports player whose contract with a team has expired

· Literary Agent, person who represents writers and their written works to publishers, theatrical producers and film producers

· Press Agent, professional publicist who acts on behalf of his or her client on all matters involving public relations

· Sports Agent, person who procures and negotiates employment and endorsement deals for a player

· Talent Agent or booking Agent, person who finds jobs for actors, musicians and models, etc., in various entertainment businesses

· Foreign Agent, person representing the interests of foreign powers, mandated by the Foreign Agents Registration Act to be identified to the American public

· Patent Agent or patent attorney, person who has the specialized qualifications necessary for representing clients in obtaining patents and acting in all matters and procedures relating to patent law and practice

· Real estate Agent or real estate broker, person who acts as an intermediary between sellers and buyers of real estate

· Travel Agent, person who works on behalf of a travel agency

· Tuition Agent, person who works on behalf of a tuition agency, specializing in introducing tutors to students requiring help in the academic area

· Yacht Agent or yacht broker, specialist who acts as a representative for the sale of a yacht or boat

· Agent , actor and decision maker in a model

· Homo economicus, concept in some economic theories of humans as rational and broadly self-interested actors

· Agent-Based Computational Economics, computational study of economic processes modeled as dynamic systems of interacting Agents

· Rational Agent, entity which has clear preferences, models uncertainty via expected values, and always chooses to perform the action that results in the optimal outcome for itself from among all feasible actions

· Representative Agent, refers to the typical decision-maker of a certain type

· A pharmacological Agent is a chemical substance with pharmacological or biological activity, i.e., a pharmaceutical drug

303

· Agent Orange, code name for an herbicide and defoliant
· Biological Agent, infectious disease or toxin that can be used in bioterrorism or biological warfare
· Chemical warfare, involves using the toxic properties of chemical substances as weapons to kill, injure, or incapacitate an enemy

· Blister Agent or vesicant, chemical compound that causes severe skin, eye and mucosal pain and irritation
· Blood Agent or cyanogen Agent, chemical compound carried by the blood for distribution throughout the body
· Incapacitating Agent, Agent that produces temporary physiological or mental effects, or both, which will render individuals incapable of concerted effort in the performance of their assigned duties
· Nerve Agent or nerve gases, class of phosphorus-containing organic chemicals (organophosphates) that disrupt the mechanism by which nerves transfer messages to organs
· Pulmonary Agent or choking Agent, chemical weapon Agent designed to impede a victim`s ability to breathe
· Riot control Agent, less-lethal lachrymatory Agents used for riot control

· Agent (grammar), the participant of a situation that carries out the action in this situation; also the name of the thematic role (also known as the thematic relation)
· Agent noun (or nomen Agentis), word that is derived from another word denoting an action, and that identifies an entity that does that action

· Agent architecture, blueprint for software Agents and intelligent control systems, depicting the arrangement of components
· Agent-based model, computational model for simulating the actions and interactions of autonomous individuals with a view to assessing their effects on the system as a whole
· Intelligent Agent, autonomous entity which observes and acts upon an environment and directs its activity towards achieving goals
· Software Agent, piece of software that acts for a user or other program in a relationship of agency

· Forté Agent, email and Usenet news client used on the Windows operating system
· User Agent, the client application used with a particular network protocol

305

· Agent 47, fictional character and protagonist in the Hitman video-game series.
· Agent 212, name of a humorous Belgian comic about a large police officer
· Agent , group of characters in the series
· Agent (video game), currently in development by Rockstar North for the Playstation 3
· The Agent (film), 1922 film featuring Oliver Hardy
· Secret Agent (1936 film), British film directed by Alfred Hitchcock
· Agent, version of The Mole (TV series) that aired in Poland on TVN
· The Agents, superhuman characters in Seven Samurai 20XX
· Agents (band), a Finnish schlager/rock`n`roll band .

Opportunities

`opportunities (Let`s Make Lots of Money)` is a song by UK synthpop duo Pet Shop Boys, released as a single in 1985 and then in 1986, gaining greater popularity in both the UK and U.S. with its second release.

Written as a satire of Thatcherism and its embodiment in conspicuous consumption and yuppies in the United Kingdom during the 1980s, the song`s indirect attack on its subject matter has come to exemplify the Pet Shop Boys as ironists in their songwriting.

The song was written during the Pet Shop Boys` formative years, in 1983. According to Neil Tennant, the main lyrical concept came while in a recording studio in Camden Town when Chris Lowe asked him to make up a lyric based around the line `Let`s make lots of money`.

Publicity

Publicity is the deliberate attempt to manage the public`s perception of a subject. The subjects of Publicity include people (for example, politicians and performing artists), goods and services, organizations of all kinds, and works of art or entertainment.

From a marketing perspective, Publicity is one component of promotion.

Commission

The Health and Safety Commission (HSC), was a United Kingdom non-departmental public body. The HSC was created by the Health and Safety at Work etc. Act 1974 (HSWA).

Promoter

In order for transcription to take place, the enzyme that synthesizes RNA, known as RNA polymerase, must attach to the DNA near a gene. Promoters contain specific DNA sequences and response elements which provide a binding site for RNA polymerase and for proteins called transcription factors that recruit RNA polymerase.

· In bacteria, the Promoter is recognized by RNA polymerase and an associated sigma factor, which in turn are often brought to the Promoter DNA by an activator protein binding to its own DNA binding site nearby.

· In eukaryotes, the process is more complicated, and at least seven different factors are necessary for the binding of an RNA polymerase II to the Promoter.

Promoters represent critical elements that can work in concert with other regulatory regions (enhancers, silencers, boundary elements/insulators) to direct the level of transcription of a given gene.

Tours

Tours is a city in central France, the capital of the Indre-et-Loire department.

It is located on the lower reaches of the river Loire, between Orléans and the Atlantic coast. Touraine, the region around Tours, is known for its wines, the alleged perfection (as perceived by some speakers) of its local spoken French, and for the famous Battle of Tours in 732. It is also the site of the cycling race Paris-Tours.

Competition

Co-operative Competition is based upon promoting mutual survival - `everyone wins`. Adam Smith`s `invisible hand` is a process where individuals compete to improve their level of happiness but compete in a cooperative manner through peaceful exchange and without violating other people. Cooperative Competition focuses individuals/groups/organisms against the environment.

Revenue

Revenue is a crucial part of financial analysis. A company`s performance is measured to the extent to which its asset inflows (revenues) compare with its asset outflows (expenses). Net Income is the result of this equation, but revenue typically enjoys equal attention during a standard earnings call.

Technology

Technology is a broad concept that deals with human as well as other animal species` usage and knowledge of tools and crafts, and how it affects a species` ability to control and adapt to its environment. Technology is a term with origins in the Greek technología -- téchnÄ“ (τἰχνη), `craft` and -logía (-λογî̄ α), the study of something, or the branch of knowledge of a discipline. However, a strict definition is elusive; `Technology` can refer to material objects of use to humanity, such as machines, hardware or utensils, but can also encompass broader themes, including systems, methods of organization, and techniques.

Amenities

In the contexts of real estate and lodging, amenities are any tangible or intangible benefits of a property, especially those which increase the attractiveness or value of the property or which contribute to its comfort or convenience.

Tangible amenities might include parks, swimming pools, health club facilities, party rooms, guest rooms (lodgings), theater or media rooms, bike paths, community centers, doormen, oyster bars or garages, for example.

Intangible amenities might include a `pleasant view` or aspect, low crime rates, or a `sun-lit living room velu`, which all add to the living comforts of the property.

Chapter 27. Professional Meeting Management

Meeting	In a Meeting, two or more people come together for the purpose of discussing a (usually) predetermined topic such as business or community event planning, often in a formal setting.
	In addition to coming together physically (in real life, face to face), communication lines and equipment can also be set up to have a discussion between people at different locations, e.g. a conference call or an e-Meeting.
	In organizations, Meetings are an important vehicle for personal contact.
Yield	Yield is the compound rate of return that includes the effect of reinvesting interest or dividends.
	To the right is an example of a stock investment of one share purchased at the beginning of the year for $100.
	· The quarterly dividend is reinvested at the quarter-end stock price. · The number of shares purchased each quarter = ($ Dividend)/($ Stock Price). · The final investment value of $103.02 is a 3.02% Yield on the initial investment of $100. This is the compound Yield, and this return can be considered to be the return on the investment of $100.
	To calculate the rate of return, the investor includes the reinvested dividends in the total investment. The investor received a total of $4.06 in dividends over the year, all of which were reinvested, so the investment amount increased by $4.06.
	· Total Investment = Cost Basis = $100 + $4.06 = $104.06. · Capital gain/loss = $103.02 - $104.06 = -$1.04 (a capital loss) · ($4.06 dividends - $1.04 capital loss) / $104.06 total investment = 2.9% ROI
	The disadvantage of this ROI calculation is that it does not take into account the fact that not all the money was invested during the entire year (the dividend reinvestments occurred throughout the year).
Business	A Business (, enterprise or firm) is a legally recognized organization designed to provide goods and/or services to consumers. Businesses are predominant in capitalist economies, most being privately owned and formed to earn profit that will increase the wealth of its owners and grow the Business itself. The owners and operators of a Business have as one of their main objectives the receipt or generation of a financial return in exchange for work and acceptance of risk.

Chapter 27. Professional Meeting Management

SMART	SMART is a mnemonic used in project management at the project objective setting stage. It is a way of evaluating the objectives or goals for an individual project. The term is also in common usage in performance management, whereby goals and targets set for employees must fulfill the criteria.
Request for proposal	A Request for proposal is an invitation for suppliers, often through a bidding process, to submit a proposal on a specific commodity or service. A bidding process is one of the best methods for leveraging a company's negotiating ability and purchasing power with suppliers. The Request for proposal process brings structure to the procurement decision and allows the risks and benefits to be identified clearly upfront.
Proposals	Proposals is a play by Neil Simon. A nostalgic memory play, proposals recalls one idyllic afternoon in the summer of 1953, the last time the Hines clan gathers at its retreat in the Poconos. Clemma, the family's housekeeper (and the story's narrator), dreads a visit from the husband who deserted her years before.
Price	Price in economics and business is the result of an exchange and from that trade we assign a numerical monetary value to a good, service or asset. If Alice trades Bob 4 apples for an orange, the Price of an orange is 4 apples. Inversely, the Price of an apple is 1/4 oranges.
Cost	In business, retail, and accounting, a Cost is the value of money that has been used up to produce something, and hence is not available for use anymore. In economics, a Cost is an alternative that is given up as a result of a decision. In business, the Cost may be one of acquisition, in which case the amount of money expended to acquire it is counted as Cost.
Revenue	Revenue is a crucial part of financial analysis. A company's performance is measured to the extent to which its asset inflows (revenues) compare with its asset outflows (expenses). Net Income is the result of this equation, but revenue typically enjoys equal attention during a standard earnings call.
University	A university is an institution of higher education and research, which grants academic degrees in a variety of subjects. A university provides both undergraduate education and postgraduate education. The word university is derived from the Latin universitas magistrorum et scholarium, roughly meaning `community of teachers and scholars`.
Procedure	A procedure is a specified series of actions or operations which have to be executed in the same manner in order to always obtain the same result under the same circumstances (for example, emergency procedures). Less precisely speaking, this word can indicate a sequence of activities, tasks, steps, decisions, calculations and processes, that when undertaken in the sequence laid down produces the described result, product or outcome. A procedure usually induces a change.

315

Chapter 27. Professional Meeting Management

Time	Time is a component of the measuring system used to sequence events, to compare the durations of events and the intervals between them, and to quantify the motions of objects. Time has been a major subject of religion, philosophy, and science, but defining it in a non-controversial manner applicable to all fields of study has consistently eluded the greatest scholars. In physics and other sciences, Time is considered one of the few fundamental quantities.
Outsourcing	Outsourcing is subcontracting a service, such as product design or manufacturing, to a third-party company. The decision whether to outsource or to do inhouse is often based upon achieving a lower production cost, making better use of available resources, focussing energy on the core competencies of a particular business, or just making more efficient use of labor, capital, information technology or land resources. It is essentially a division of labour.
Order	An order in a market such as a stock market, bond market or commodity market is an instruction from a customer to a broker to buy or sell on the exchange. These instructions can be simple or complicated. There are some standard instructions for such orders.
Planning	Planning in organizations and public policy is both the organizational process of creating and maintaining a plan; and the psychological process of thinking about the activities required to create a desired goal on some scale. As such, it is a fundamental property of intelligent behavior. This thought process is essential to the creation and refinement of a plan, or integration of it with other plans, that is, it combines forecasting of developments with the preparation of scenarios of how to react to them.
Specification	A Specification is an explicit set of requirements to be satisfied by a material, product, or service. In engineering, manufacturing, and business, it is vital for suppliers, purchasers, and users of materials, products, or services to understand and agree upon all requirements. A Specification is a type of a standard which is often referenced by a contract or procurement document.
Conference	A Conference is a meeting of people that `confer` about a topic.

· Academic Conference, in science and academia, a formal event where researchers present results, workshops, and other activities.

· Business Conference, organized to discuss business-related matters best effected there.

· News Conference, an announcement to the press (print, radio, television) with the expectation of questions, about the announced matter, following.

· Settlement Conference, a meeting between the plaintiff and the respondent in lawsuit, wherein they try to settle their dispute without proceeding to trial

· Conference (sports), a grouping of geographically-related teams

· Conference call, in telecommunications, a `multi-party call`

· Conference hall, room where Conferences are held

· Football Conference, an English football league

· In the Netherlands, a solo cabaret act, a type of stand-up comedy lasting one to two hours

· Parent-teacher Conference, a meeting with a child`s teacher to discuss grades and school performance.

· UnConference .

Call for bids	A Call for bids or call for tenders or invitation to tender (ITT) (often called tender for short) is a special procedure for generating competing offers from different bidders looking to obtain an award of business activity in works, supply). Open tenders, open calls for tenders, or advertised tenders are open to all vendors or contractors who can guarantee performance.
Hurricane Katrina	Hurricane Katrina of the 2005 Atlantic hurricane season was the costliest hurricane, as well as one of the five deadliest, in the history of the United States. Among recorded Atlantic hurricanes, it was the sixth strongest overall. Hurricane Katrina formed over the Bahamas on August 23, 2005 and crossed southern Florida as a moderate Category 1 hurricane, causing some deaths and flooding there before strengthening rapidly in the Gulf of Mexico.
Room	A Room, in architecture, is any distinguishable space within a structure. Most typically a Room is separated by interior walls from other spaces or passageways; moreover, it is separated by an exterior wall from outdoor areas, sometimes with a door. Historically the use of Rooms dates at least to early Minoan cultures about 2200 BC, where excavations on Santorini, Greece at Akrotiri reveal clearly defined Rooms within structures.
Pirate	Pirate or piracy may also refer to:

Chapter 27. Professional Meeting Management

· Aircraft hijacking
· Copyright infringement
· Misappropriation of traditional knowledge, the attaining of legal ownership over a culture`s long-held practices or lore
· Oyster Pirate, an oyster poacher
· Patent infringement
· Pirate radio

· The Pirate, a 1948 American musical film
· The Pirate (1984 film), a 1984 French film
· Pirates , an adventure/comedy directed by Roman Polanski
· Pirates (2005 film), a pornographic film
· Pirates of the Caribbean (film series)

· Sid Meier`s Pirates!, an 1987 computer game

· Sid Meier`s Pirates! (2004 video game), a remake of the 1987 game
· Pirates! (role-playing game)
· Pirates: The Key of Dreams, a 2008 video game for Wii
· Pirates: Duels on the High Seas, a 2008 video game for Nintendo DS
· Pirates Constructible Strategy Game, a tabletop game
· Pirates of the Burning Sea, (MMORPG)

· The Pirates, an opera by Stephen Storace
· Johnny Kidd ' The Pirates, a British musical group

· The Pirate (novel), an 1821 novel by Sir Walter Scott
· `The Pirate` (short story), a science fiction story by Poul Anderson
· Piracy (comics)
· The Pirate, a 1974 novel by Harold Robbins

· USS Pirate, the name of more than one United States Navy ship

United States

Chapter 27. Professional Meeting Management

· Pittsburgh Pirates, an American baseball team
· Portland Pirates, an American hockey team
· East Carolina Pirates, the sports teams of East Carolina University
· Hampton Pirates, the sports teams of Hampton University
· Pittsburgh Pirates (NHL), an American hockey team existing from 1925-1930
· Pittsburgh Steelers, an American football team, known as the Pittsburgh Pirates from 1933-1939
· Seton Hall Pirates, the sports teams of Seton Hall University

United Kingdom

· Croydon Pirates, a baseball team
· Cornish Pirates, a British rugby team
· East Kilbride Pirates, a British American football team
· Poole Pirates, a British motorcycle speedway team
· Bristol Rovers F.C., an English football team, nicknamed the Pirates

Elsewhere

· Orlando Pirates FC, a South African football team

· Pirate Party various political parties around the world
· Lego Pirates
· Space Pirate, a character archetype in science fiction
· Pirate (R-Class Sloop), a landmark in South Lake Union, Seattle .

Program | The Program (or Project) Evaluation and Review Technique, commonly abbreviated PERT, is a model for project management designed to analyze and represent the tasks involved in completing a given project.

PERT is a method to analyze the involved tasks in completing a given project, especially the time needed to complete each task, and identifying the minimum time needed to complete the total project.

PERT was developed primarily to simplify the planning and scheduling of large and complex projects.

Chapter 27. Professional Meeting Management

Dot.com bubble

The `Dot.com bubble` (or) was a speculative bubble covering roughly 1998-2001 (with a climax on March 10, 2000 with the NASDAQ peaking at 5132.52) during which stock markets in Western nations saw their equity value rise rapidly from growth in the more recent Internet sector and related fields. While the latter part was a boom and bust cycle, the Internet boom sometimes is meant to refer to the steady commercial growth of the Internet with the advent of the world wide web as exemplified by the first release of the Mosaic web browser in 1993 and continuing through the 1990s.

The period was marked by the founding (and, in many cases, spectacular failure) of a group of new Internet-based companies commonly referred to as dot-coms.

Chapter 28. Exhibition (Trade Show) Management

Consumer	Consumer is a broad label for any individuals or households that use goods and services generated within the economy. The concept of a Consumer is used in different contexts, so that the usage and significance of the term may vary. Typically when business people and economists talk of Consumers they are talking about person as Consumer, an aggregated commodity item with little individuality other than that expressed in the buy/not-buy decision.
Supplier	A `supply chain is the system of organizations, people, technology, activities, information and resources involved in moving a product or service from supplier to customer. Supply chain activities transform natural resources, raw materials and components into a finished product that is delivered to the end customer. In sophisticated supply chain systems, used products may re-enter the supply chain at any point where residual value is recyclable.
Cost	In business, retail, and accounting, a Cost is the value of money that has been used up to produce something, and hence is not available for use anymore. In economics, a Cost is an alternative that is given up as a result of a decision. In business, the Cost may be one of acquisition, in which case the amount of money expended to acquire it is counted as Cost.
Anecdotal value	In economics, Anecdotal value refers to the primarily social and political value of an anecdote or anecdotal evidence in promoting understanding of a social, cultural, in the last several decades the evaluation of anecdotes has received sustained academic scrutiny from economists and scholars such as S.G. Checkland (on David Ricardo), Steven Novella, Hollis Robbins, R. Charleton, Kwamena Kwansah-Aidoo, and others; these academics seek to quantify the value inherent in the deployment of anecdotes. More recently, economists studying choice models have begun assessing Anecdotal value in the context of framing; Kahneman and Tversky suggest that choice models may be contingent on stories or anecdotes that frame or influence choice.
Recession	In economics, a Recession is a general slowdown in economic activity over a sustained period of time, or a business cycle contraction. During Recession s, many macroeconomic indicators vary in a similar way. Production as measured by Gross Domestic Product (GDP), employment, investment spending, capacity utilization, household incomes and business profits all fall during Recession s.
Business	A Business (, enterprise or firm) is a legally recognized organization designed to provide goods and/or services to consumers. Businesses are predominant in capitalist economies, most being privately owned and formed to earn profit that will increase the wealth of its owners and grow the Business itself. The owners and operators of a Business have as one of their main objectives the receipt or generation of a financial return in exchange for work and acceptance of risk.
Call for bids	A Call for bids or call for tenders or invitation to tender (ITT) (often called tender for short) is a special procedure for generating competing offers from different bidders looking to obtain an award of business activity in works, supply).

Chapter 28. Exhibition (Trade Show) Management

	Open tenders, open calls for tenders, or advertised tenders are open to all vendors or contractors who can guarantee performance.
General contractor	A general contractor is a group or individual that contracts with another organization or individual (the owner) for the construction, renovation or demolition of a building, road or other structure. A general contractor is defined as such if it is the signatory as the builder of the prime construction contract for the project. A general contractor is responsible for the means and methods to be used in the construction execution of the project in accordance with the contract documents.
Taxes	To tax is to impose a financial charge or other levy upon an individual or legal entity by a state or the functional equivalent of a state. Taxes are also imposed by many subnational entities. Taxes consist of direct tax or indirect tax, and may be paid in money or as its labour equivalent .
Request for proposal	A Request for proposal is an invitation for suppliers, often through a bidding process, to submit a proposal on a specific commodity or service. A bidding process is one of the best methods for leveraging a company`s negotiating ability and purchasing power with suppliers. The Request for proposal process brings structure to the procurement decision and allows the risks and benefits to be identified clearly upfront.
Proposals	Proposals is a play by Neil Simon. A nostalgic memory play, proposals recalls one idyllic afternoon in the summer of 1953, the last time the Hines clan gathers at its retreat in the Poconos. Clemma, the family`s housekeeper (and the story`s narrator), dreads a visit from the husband who deserted her years before.
Continuing education	Continuing education is an all encompassing term within a broad spectrum of post-secondary learning activities and programs. The term is used mainly in the United States. Recognized forms of post-secondary learning activities within the domain include: degree credit courses by non-traditional students, non-degree career training, workforce training, formal personal enrichment courses (both on-campus and online) self-directed learning (such as through Internet interest groups, clubs or personal research activities) and experiential learning as applied to problem solving.

Chapter 28. Exhibition (Trade Show) Management

Technology	Technology is a broad concept that deals with human as well as other animal species` usage and knowledge of tools and crafts, and how it affects a species` ability to control and adapt to its environment. Technology is a term with origins in the Greek technología -- téchnÄ" (τî̀χvη), `craft` and -logía (-λογî̀ α), the study of something, or the branch of knowledge of a discipline. However, a strict definition is elusive; `Technology` can refer to material objects of use to humanity, such as machines, hardware or utensils, but can also encompass broader themes, including systems, methods of organization, and techniques.
Amenities	In the contexts of real estate and lodging, amenities are any tangible or intangible benefits of a property, especially those which increase the attractiveness or value of the property or which contribute to its comfort or convenience. Tangible amenities might include parks, swimming pools, health club facilities, party rooms, guest rooms (lodgings), theater or media rooms, bike paths, community centers, doormen, oyster bars or garages, for example. Intangible amenities might include a `pleasant view` or aspect, low crime rates, or a `sun-lit living room velu`, which all add to the living comforts of the property.
Point	In typography, a point is the smallest unit of measure, being a subdivision of the larger pica. It is commonly abbreviated as pt. The traditional printer`s point, from the era of hot metal typesetting and presswork, varied between 0.18 and 0.4 mm depending on various definitions of the foot. Today, the traditional point has been supplanted by the desktop publishing point (also called the PostScript point), which has been rounded to an even 72 points to the inch (1 point = $^{127}/_{360}$ mm ≈ 0.353 mm).
Maxima	In mathematics, maxima and minima, known collectively as extrema (singular: extremum), are the largest value (maximum) or smallest value (minimum), that a function takes in a point either within a given neighbourhood (local extremum) or on the function domain in its entirety (global extremum). Throughout, a Point refers to an input (x), while a value refers to an output (y): one distinguishing between the maximum value and the point (or points) at which it occurs. A real-valued function f defined on the real line is said to have a local (or relative) maximum point at the point x^*, if there exists some ε > 0, such that $f(x^*) \geq f(x)$ when $\left\lvert x - x^* \right\rvert < \varepsilon$.

Chapter 28. Exhibition (Trade Show) Management

Chapter 29. Special Events Management

Public relations	Public relations is the practice of managing the communication between an organization and its publics. Public relations gains an organization or individual exposure to their audiences using topics of public interest and news items that do not require direct payment. Because Public relations places exposure in credible third-party outlets, it offers a third-party legitimacy that advertising does not have.
Business	A Business (, enterprise or firm) is a legally recognized organization designed to provide goods and/or services to consumers. Businesses are predominant in capitalist economies, most being privately owned and formed to earn profit that will increase the wealth of its owners and grow the Business itself. The owners and operators of a Business have as one of their main objectives the receipt or generation of a financial return in exchange for work and acceptance of risk.
Parade	A Parade is a procession of people, usually organized along a street, often in costume, and often accompanied by marching bands, floats or , but are usually celebrations of some kind. In Britain the term Parade is usually reserved for either military Parades or other occasions where participants march in formation; for celebratory occasions the word procession is more usual.
Festival	A festival is an event, usually and ordinarily staged by a local community, which centers on some unique aspect of that community.
	Among many religions, a feast is a set of celebrations in honour of God or gods. A feast and a festival are historically interchangeable.
Promotion	Promotion involves disseminating information about a product, product line, brand, or company. It is one of the four key aspects of the marketing mix. (The other three elements are product marketing, pricing, and distribution). P>Promotion is generally sub-divided into two parts:
	· Above the line Promotion: Promotion in the media (e.g. TV, radio, newspapers, Internet and Mobile Phones) in which the advertiser pays an advertising agency to place the ad · Below the line Promotion: All other Promotion. Much of this is intended to be subtle enough for the consumer to be unaware that Promotion is taking place. E.g. sponsorship, product placement, endorsements, sales Promotion, merchandising, direct mail, personal selling, public relations, trade shows
Organization	Management is interested in organization mainly from an instrumental point of view. For a company, organization is a means to an end to achieve its goals.
	Among the theories that are or have been most influential are:

· Pyramids or hierarchies
· Committees or juries
· Matrix organizations
· Ecologies

A hierarchy exemplifies an arrangement with a leader who leads leaders. This arrangement is often associated with bureaucracy.

Social	The term social refers to a characteristic of living organisms (humans in particular, though biologists also apply the term to populations of other animals). It always refers to the interaction of organisms with other organisms and to their collective co-existence, irrespective of whether they are aware of it or not, and irrespective of whether the interaction is voluntary or involuntary. In the absence of agreement about its meaning, the term `ps` is used in many different senses and regarded as a [[]], referringse among other things to: · Attitudes, orientations, or behaviours which take the interests, intentions, or needs of other people into account (in contrast to anti-social behaviour);has played some role in defining the idea or the principle. For instance terms like social realism, social justice, social constructivism, social psychology and social capital imply that there is some social process involved or considered, a process that is not there in regular, `non-social`, realism, justice, constructivism, psychology, or capital.
Safety	Safety is the state of being `safe` , the condition of being protected against physical, social, spiritual, financial, political, emotional, occupational, psychological, educational or other types or consequences of failure, damage, error, accidents, harm or any other event which could be considered non-desirable. This can take the form of being protected from the event or from exposure to something that causes health or economical losses. It can include protection of people or of possessions.
September	September Â·) is the ninth month of the year in the Gregorian Calendar and one of four Gregorian months with 30 days. In Latin, septem means `seven` and septimus means `seventh`; September was in fact the seventh month of the Roman calendar until 153 BC, when there was a calendar reform from the month of the Ides of March to the Kalends, or January 1. September marks the beginning of the ecclesiastical year in the Eastern Orthodox Church.

Chapter 29. Special Events Management

Terrorism	Terrorism, according to the Oxford English Dictionary is `A policy intended to strike with terror those against whom it is adopted; the employment of methods of intimidation; the fact of terrorizing or condition of being terrorized.` At present, there is no internationally agreed upon definition of terrorism. Common definitions of terrorism refer only to those acts which are intended to create fear (terror), (2) are perpetrated for an ideological goal (as opposed to a materialistic goal or a lone attack), and (3) deliberately target (or disregard the safety of) non-combatants. Some definitions also include acts of unlawful violence or unconventional warfare.
Trend	A trend is a line of general direction of movement, a prevaling tendency of inclination, a style or preference, a line of development, `trend` is a synonym to `tendency`. A fad is a practice or interest followed for a time with exaggerated zeal.
Risk	Risk concerns the expected value of one or more results of one or more future events. Technically, the value of those results may be positive or negative. However, general usage tends focus only on potential harm that may arise from a future event, which may accrue either from incurring a cost (`downside Risk`) or by failing to attain some benefit (`upside Risk`).
Risk management	Example of Risk management: NASA`s illustration showing high impact risk areas for the International Space Station`. Risk management is the identification, assessment, and prioritization of risks followed by coordinated and economical application of resources to minimize, monitor, and control the probability and/or impact of unfortunate events. Risks can come from uncertainty in financial markets, project failures, legal liabilities, credit risk, accidents, natural causes and disasters as well as deliberate attacks from an adversary. Several Risk management standards have been developed including the Project Management Institute, the National Institute of Science and Technology, actuarial societies, and ISO standards.
Planning	Planning in organizations and public policy is both the organizational process of creating and maintaining a plan; and the psychological process of thinking about the activities required to create a desired goal on some scale. As such, it is a fundamental property of intelligent behavior. This thought process is essential to the creation and refinement of a plan, or integration of it with other plans, that is, it combines forecasting of developments with the preparation of scenarios of how to react to them.
Career	Career is a term defined by the Oxford English Dictionary as an individual`s `course or progress through life `. It is usually considered to pertain to remunerative work (and sometimes also formal education). The etymology of the term is somewhat ironic in that it comes from the Latin word carrera, which means race .
Opportunities	`opportunities (Let`s Make Lots of Money)` is a song by UK synthpop duo Pet Shop Boys, released as a single in 1985 and then in 1986, gaining greater popularity in both the UK and U.S. with its second release.

Written as a satire of Thatcherism and its embodiment in conspicuous consumption and yuppies in the United Kingdom during the 1980s, the song`s indirect attack on its subject matter has come to exemplify the Pet Shop Boys as ironists in their songwriting.

The song was written during the Pet Shop Boys` formative years, in 1983. According to Neil Tennant, the main lyrical concept came while in a recording studio in Camden Town when Chris Lowe asked him to make up a lyric based around the line `Let`s make lots of money`.

Marketing

Marketing is a `social and managerial process by which individuals and groups obtain what they need and want through creating and exchanging products and values with others.` It is an integrated process through which companies create value for customers and build strong customer relationships in order to capture value from customers in return.

marketing is used to create the customer, to keep the customer and to satisfy the customer. With the customer as the focus of its activities, it can be concluded that marketing management is one of the major components of business management.

Industry

An Industry is the manufacturing of a good or service within a category. Although Industry is a broad term for any kind of economic production, in economics and urban planning Industry is a synonym for the secondary sector, which is a type of economic activity involved in the manufacturing of raw materials into goods and products.

There are four key industrial economic sectors: the primary sector, largely raw material extraction industries such as mining and farming; the secondary sector, involving refining, construction, and manufacturing; the tertiary sector, which deals with services and distribution of manufactured goods; and the quaternary sector, a relatively new type of knowledge Industry focusing on technological research, design and development such as computer programming, and biochemistry.

Chapter 30. Planning Your Hospitality Career

Career	Career is a term defined by the Oxford English Dictionary as an individual`s `course or progress through life `. It is usually considered to pertain to remunerative work (and sometimes also formal education). The etymology of the term is somewhat ironic in that it comes from the Latin word carrera, which means race .
Evaluation	Pseudo-Evaluation Politically controlled and public relations studies are based on an objectivist epistemology from an elite perspective. Although both of these approaches seek to misrepresent value interpretations about some object, they go about it a bit differently. Information obtained through politically controlled studies is released or withheld to meet the special interests of the holder.
Planning	Planning in organizations and public policy is both the organizational process of creating and maintaining a plan; and the psychological process of thinking about the activities required to create a desired goal on some scale. As such, it is a fundamental property of intelligent behavior. This thought process is essential to the creation and refinement of a plan, or integration of it with other plans, that is, it combines forecasting of developments with the preparation of scenarios of how to react to them.
Personal	A personal ad is an item or notice traditionally in the newspaper, similar to a classified ad but personal in nature. In British English it is also commonly known as an advert in a lonely hearts column. With its rise in popularity, the World Wide Web has also become a common medium for personals, commonly referred to as online dating.
Mission statement	A mission statement is a formal short written statement of the purpose of a company or organization. The mission statement should guide the actions of the organization, spell out its overall goal, provide a sense of direction, and guide decision-making. It provides `the framework or context within which the companyÂ´s strategies are formulated.` Historically it is associated with Christian religious groups; indeed, for many years a missionary was assumed to be a person on a specifically religious mission.
Professional	A professional is a member of a vocation founded upon specialised educational training. The word professional traditionally means a person who has obtained a degree in a professional field. The term professional is used more generally to denote a white collar working person, or a person who performs commercially in a field typically reserved for hobbyists or amateurs.

341

Chapter 30. Planning Your Hospitality Career

Career ladder	The term `career ladder` is a metaphor or buzzword used to denote vertical job promotion. In business and human resources management, the ladder typically describes the progression from entry level positions to higher levels of pay, skill, responsibility, or authority. This metaphor is spatially oriented, and frequently used to denote upward mobility within a stratified promotion model.
Glass ceiling	In economics, the term Glass ceiling refers to situations where the advancement of a qualified person within the hierarchy of an organization is stopped at a lower level because of some form of discrimination, most commonly sexism or racism, but since the term was coined, `Glass ceiling` has also come to describe the limited advancement of the deaf, blind, disabled, and aged. It is believed to be an unofficial, invisible barrier that prevents women and minorities from advancing in businesses. This situation is referred to as a `ceiling` as there is a limitation blocking upward advancement, and `glass` (transparent) because the limitation is not immediately apparent and is normally an unwritten and unofficial policy.
Women	A woman (irregular plural: women) is a female human. The term woman is usually reserved for an adult, with the term girl being the usual term for a female child or adolescent. However, the term woman is also sometimes used to identify a female human, regardless of age, as in phrases such as `women`s rights`.
Professional development	Professional development refers to skills and knowledge attained for both personal development and career advancement. professional development encompasses all types of facilitated learning opportunities, ranging from college degrees to formal coursework, conferences and informal learning opportunities situated in practice. It has been described as intensive and collaborative, ideally incorporating an evaluative stage There are a variety of approaches to professional development, including consultation, coaching, communities of practice, lesson study, mentoring, reflective supervision and technical assistance.

Chapter 31. The Job Search: Your First Professional Position

Career	Career is a term defined by the Oxford English Dictionary as an individual`s `course or progress through life `. It is usually considered to pertain to remunerative work (and sometimes also formal education).
	The etymology of the term is somewhat ironic in that it comes from the Latin word carrera, which means race .
Evaluation	Pseudo-Evaluation
	Politically controlled and public relations studies are based on an objectivist epistemology from an elite perspective. Although both of these approaches seek to misrepresent value interpretations about some object, they go about it a bit differently. Information obtained through politically controlled studies is released or withheld to meet the special interests of the holder.
Planning	Planning in organizations and public policy is both the organizational process of creating and maintaining a plan; and the psychological process of thinking about the activities required to create a desired goal on some scale. As such, it is a fundamental property of intelligent behavior. This thought process is essential to the creation and refinement of a plan, or integration of it with other plans, that is, it combines forecasting of developments with the preparation of scenarios of how to react to them.
GROW model	The GROW model (or process) is a technique for problem solving or goal setting. It was developed in the UK and used extensively in the corporate coaching market in the late 1980s and 1990s. There have been many claims to authorship of GROW as a way of achieving goals and solving problems.
Internships	Internships are often referred to as `sandwich placements` in the UK and are validated work experienced opportunity as part of a degree program. University staff give students access to vacancies and students apply direct to employers. Some universities hold fairs and exhibitions to encourage students to consider the option and to enable students to meet potential employers.
Professional	A professional is a member of a vocation founded upon specialised educational training.
	The word professional traditionally means a person who has obtained a degree in a professional field. The term professional is used more generally to denote a white collar working person, or a person who performs commercially in a field typically reserved for hobbyists or amateurs.
Employment	Employment is a contract between two parties, one being the employer and the other being the employee. An employee may be defined as: `A person in the service of another under any contract of hire, express or implied, oral or written, where the employer has the power or right to control and direct the employee in the material details of how the work is to be performed.` Black`s Law Dictionary page 471 (5th ed. 1979).

345

In a commercial setting, the employer conceives of a productive activity, generally with the intention of generating a profit, and the employee contributes labour to the enterprise, usually in return for payment of wages.

Organization	Management is interested in organization mainly from an instrumental point of view. For a company, organization is a means to an end to achieve its goals.

Among the theories that are or have been most influential are:

· Pyramids or hierarchies
· Committees or juries
· Matrix organizations
· Ecologies

A hierarchy exemplifies an arrangement with a leader who leads leaders. This arrangement is often associated with bureaucracy.

Research	Research is defined as human activity based on intellectual application in the investigation of matter. The primary purpose for applied research is discovering, interpreting, and the development of methods and systems for the advancement of human knowledge on a wide variety of scientific matters of our world and the universe. research can use the scientific method, but need not do so.
Cover letter	A Cover letter or covering letter or motivation letter or motivational letter or letter of motivation is a letter of introduction attached to
Choice	There are four types of decisions, although they can be expressed in different ways. Brian Tracy, who often uses enumerated lists in his talks, breaks them down into:

· Command decisions, which can only be made by you, as the `Commander in Chief`; or owner of a company.
· Delegated decisions, which may be made by anyone, such as the color of the bike shed, and should be delegated, as the decision must be made but the Choice is inconsequential.
· Avoided decisions, where the outcome could be so severe that the Choice should not be made, as the consequences can not be recovered from if the wrong Choice is made. This will most likely result in negative actions, such as death.
· `No-brainer` decisions, where the Choice is so obvious that only one Choice can reasonably be made.

Chapter 31. The Job Search: Your First Professional Position

	A fifth type, however, or fourth if three and four are combined as one type, is the collaborative decision, which should be made in consultation with, and by agreement of others.
Upmarket	Upmarket (or high-end) commodities are products, services or real estate targeted at high-income consumers. Examples of products would include items from Ferrari, Mercedes-Benz, Hammacher -Schlemmer, and Chanel. In the United States, Upmarket real estate areas are generally characterized by being within the city limits or a suburb of a major city, a high concentration of multi-million dollar homes (typically several hundred or more), high household incomes (generally a family average of $275,000 per year or more), an abundance of luxury boutiques, hotels, restaurants, vehicle dealerships, exclusive golf courses and nation wide familiarity on a first name basis without the inclusion of an anchor city or state.
Restaurant	A restaurant prepares and serves food and drink to customers. Meals are generally served and eaten on premises, but many restaurant s also offer take-out and food delivery services. restaurant s vary greatly in appearance and offerings, including a wide variety of cuisines and service models.
Question	A Question may be either a linguistic expression used to make a request for information
Activities	Activity may mean: · Action (philosophy), in general · the Aristotelian concept of energeia, Latinized as actus · physical activity · mental activity · Activity · Activity (UML) · Activity, an alternative name for the game charades · Activity, a task. · Activity, the ability of a piece to influence the game in chess · Activity, the rate of a catalytic reaction, such as enzyme activity, in physical chemistry and enzymology · activity (chemistry), the effective concentration of a solute for the purposes of mass action · activity (project management) · activity (radioactivity), the number of radioactive decays per second · activity (software engineering) · activity (soil mechanics) · activity diagram, a diagram representing activities in UML · Activity, a board game by Piatnik · HMS Activity, an aircraft carrier of the Royal Navy · in military parlance, a military agency or unit (e.g. Intelligence Support Activity) .

| Lee | Lee is a brand of denim jeans, first produced in 1889 in Salina, Kansas. The company is owned by VF Corporation, the largest apparel company in the world. Its headquarters are currently in Merriam near Kansas City, Kansas. |

Chapter 32. Your First Professional Position: Celebrate Success

Career	Career is a term defined by the Oxford English Dictionary as an individual's `course or progress through life `. It is usually considered to pertain to remunerative work (and sometimes also formal education). The etymology of the term is somewhat ironic in that it comes from the Latin word carrera, which means race .
Professional	A professional is a member of a vocation founded upon specialised educational training. The word professional traditionally means a person who has obtained a degree in a professional field. The term professional is used more generally to denote a white collar working person, or a person who performs commercially in a field typically reserved for hobbyists or amateurs.
Program	The Program (or Project) Evaluation and Review Technique, commonly abbreviated PERT, is a model for project management designed to analyze and represent the tasks involved in completing a given project. PERT is a method to analyze the involved tasks in completing a given project, especially the time needed to complete each task, and identifying the minimum time needed to complete the total project. PERT was developed primarily to simplify the planning and scheduling of large and complex projects.
Competency	Competence is the ability to perform a specific task, action or function successfully. Incompetence is its opposite. · Competence (biology), the ability of a cell to take up DNA · Competence (geology), the resistance of a rock against either erosion or deformation · Competence (human resources), a standardized requirement for an individual to properly perform a specific job · Competence (law), the mental capacity of an individual to participate in legal proceedings · Competency evaluation (law) · Jurisdiction, the authority of a legal body to deal with and make pronouncements on legal matters and, by implication, to administer justice within a defined area of responsibility · Linguistic competence, the ability to speak and understand language. · Communicative competence, the ability to speak and understand language. .

Chapter 32. Your First Professional Position: Celebrate Success

Human relations	Human relations Movement refers to those researchers of organizational development who study the behavior of people in groups, in particular workplace groups. It originated in the 1920s` Hawthorne studies, which examined the effects of social relations, motivation and employee satisfaction on factory productivity. The movement viewed workers in terms of their psychology and fit with companies, rather than as interchangeable parts.  `The hallmark of human-relation theories is the primacy given to organizations as human cooperative systems rather than mechanical contraptions.` George Elton Mayo stressed the following: · Natural groups, in which social aspects take precedence over functional organizational structures · Upwards communication, by which communication is two way, from worker to chief executive, as well as vice versa. · Cohesive and good leadership is needed to communicate goals and to ensure effective and coherent decision making (Wilson ' Rosenfeld, Managing Organizations, McGraw Hill Book Company, London, p.9).
Skill	· Foundation Skills: From the employer`s perspective, the Skill of knowing how to learn is cost-effective because it can mitigate the cost of retraining efforts. When workers use efficient learning strategies, they absorb and apply training more quickly, saving their employers money and time. When properly prepared, employees can use learning-to-learn techniques to distinguish between essential and nonessential information, discern patterns in information, and pinpoint the actions necessary to improve job performance.
Day	The word Day is used for several different units of time based on the rotation of the Earth around its axis. The most important one follows the apparent motion of the Sun across the sky (solar Day). The reason for this apparent motion is the rotation of the Earth around its axis, as well as the revolution of the Earth in its orbit around the Sun.
Dot.com bubble	The `Dot.com bubble` (or) was a speculative bubble covering roughly 1998-2001 (with a climax on March 10, 2000 with the NASDAQ peaking at 5132.52) during which stock markets in Western nations saw their equity value rise rapidly from growth in the more recent Internet sector and related fields. While the latter part was a boom and bust cycle, the Internet boom sometimes is meant to refer to the steady commercial growth of the Internet with the advent of the world wide web as exemplified by the first release of the Mosaic web browser in 1993 and continuing through the 1990s. The period was marked by the founding (and, in many cases, spectacular failure) of a group of new Internet-based companies commonly referred to as dot-coms.

355

Chapter 32. Your First Professional Position: Celebrate Success

Promotion	Promotion involves disseminating information about a product, product line, brand, or company. It is one of the four key aspects of the marketing mix. (The other three elements are product marketing, pricing, and distribution). P>Promotion is generally sub-divided into two parts: · Above the line Promotion: Promotion in the media (e.g. TV, radio, newspapers, Internet and Mobile Phones) in which the advertiser pays an advertising agency to place the ad · Below the line Promotion: All other Promotion. Much of this is intended to be subtle enough for the consumer to be unaware that Promotion is taking place. E.g. sponsorship, product placement, endorsements, sales Promotion, merchandising, direct mail, personal selling, public relations, trade shows
Work ethic	Work ethic is a set of values based on hard work and diligence. It is also a belief in the moral benefit of work and its ability to enhance character. An example would be the Protestant Work ethic.
NHS Together	NHS Together is a campaign alliance of the health service unions in the United Kingdom and staff associations working with the TUC, which opposes any form of competition with, the National Health Service. It is made up of several unions, including UNISON and the British Medical Association. NHS Together is a group of organisations, largely health service trade unions, opposing any reforms which would involve privatisation or extension of private sector operation within the NHS. They claim that: `We want to raise the alarm at what is happening to the NHS and to press the government for honest and open discussion about its reform agenda.
Multiple comparisons	In statistics, the multiple comparisons (or `multiple testing`) problem occurs when one considers a set, of statistical inferences simultaneously. Errors in inference, including confidence intervals that fail to include their corresponding population parameters, or hypothesis tests that incorrectly reject the null hypothesis, are more likely to occur when one considers the family as a whole. Several statistical techniques have been developed to prevent this from happening, allowing significance levels for single and multiple comparisons to be directly compared.
Business	A Business (, enterprise or firm) is a legally recognized organization designed to provide goods and/or services to consumers. Businesses are predominant in capitalist economies, most being privately owned and formed to earn profit that will increase the wealth of its owners and grow the Business itself. The owners and operators of a Business have as one of their main objectives the receipt or generation of a financial return in exchange for work and acceptance of risk.

Chapter 32. Your First Professional Position: Celebrate Success

Businesses	A business (, enterprise or firm) is a legally recognized organization designed to provide goods and/or services to consumers. Businesses are predominant in capitalist economies, most being privately owned and formed to earn profit that will increase the wealth of its owners and grow the business itself. The owners and operators of a business have as one of their main objectives the receipt or generation of a financial return in exchange for work and acceptance of risk.
Career ladder	The term `career ladder` is a metaphor or buzzword used to denote vertical job promotion. In business and human resources management, the ladder typically describes the progression from entry level positions to higher levels of pay, skill, responsibility, or authority. This metaphor is spatially oriented, and frequently used to denote upward mobility within a stratified promotion model.
Diversification	Diversification in finance is a risk management technique, related to hedging, that mixes a wide variety of investments within a portfolio. It is the spreading out investments to reduce risks. Because the fluctuations of a single security have less impact on a diverse portfolio, Diversification minimizes the risk from any one investment.
Outsourcing	Outsourcing is subcontracting a service, such as product design or manufacturing, to a third-party company. The decision whether to outsource or to do inhouse is often based upon achieving a lower production cost, making better use of available resources, focussing energy on the core competencies of a particular business, or just making more efficient use of labor, capital, information technology or land resources. It is essentially a division of labour.
Professional development	Professional development refers to skills and knowledge attained for both personal development and career advancement. professional development encompasses all types of facilitated learning opportunities, ranging from college degrees to formal coursework, conferences and informal learning opportunities situated in practice. It has been described as intensive and collaborative, ideally incorporating an evaluative stage There are a variety of approaches to professional development, including consultation, coaching, communities of practice, lesson study, mentoring, reflective supervision and technical assistance.
Merchandising	Merchandising is the methods, practices, and operations used to promote and sustain certain categories of commercial activity. In retail commerce, visual display Merchandising means maximizing merchandise sales using product design, selection, packaging, pricing, and display that stimulates consumers to spend more. This includes disciplines in pricing and discounting, physical presentation of products and displays, and the decisions about which products should be presented to which customers at what time.
Restaurant	A restaurant prepares and serves food and drink to customers. Meals are generally served and eaten on premises, but many restaurant s also offer take-out and food delivery services. restaurant s vary greatly in appearance and offerings, including a wide variety of cuisines and service models.

359

Chapter 32. Your First Professional Position: Celebrate Success

Opportunities	`opportunities (Let`s Make Lots of Money)` is a song by UK synthpop duo Pet Shop Boys, released as a single in 1985 and then in 1986, gaining greater popularity in both the UK and U.S. with its second release. Written as a satire of Thatcherism and its embodiment in conspicuous consumption and yuppies in the United Kingdom during the 1980s, the song`s indirect attack on its subject matter has come to exemplify the Pet Shop Boys as ironists in their songwriting.  The song was written during the Pet Shop Boys` formative years, in 1983. According to Neil Tennant, the main lyrical concept came while in a recording studio in Camden Town when Chris Lowe asked him to make up a lyric based around the line `Let`s make lots of money`.
The U.S.	The United States of America (commonly referred to as the United States, the U.S., the USA) is a federal constitutional republic comprising fifty states and a federal district. The country is situated mostly in central North America, where its forty-eight contiguous states and Washington, D.C., the capital district, lie between the Pacific and Atlantic Oceans, bordered by Canada to the north and Mexico to the south. The state of Alaska is in the northwest of the continent, with Canada to the east and Russia to the west across the Bering Strait.
Certification	Certification refers to the confirmation of certain characteristics of an object, person, or organization. This confirmation is often, but not always, provided by some form of external review, education, or assessment. One of the most common types of certification in modern society is professional certification, where a person is certified as being able to competently complete a job or task, usually by the passing of an examination.
Club	A Club is an association of two or more people united by a common interest or goal. A service Club, for example, exists for voluntary or charitable activities; there are Clubs devoted to hobbies and sports, social activities Clubs, political and religious Clubs, and so forth. Historically, Clubs occurred in all ancient states of which we have detailed knowledge.

Chapter 32. Your First Professional Position: Celebrate Success

Chapter 33. Entrepreneur or Intrapreneur?

Resources	Human beings are also considered to be Resources because they have the ability to change raw materials into valuable Resources. The term Human Resources can also be defined as the skills, energies, talents, abilities and knowledge that are used for the production of goods or the rendering of services. While taking into account human beings as Resources, the following things have to be kept in mind: · The size of the population · The capabilities of the individuals in that population Many Resources cannot be consumed in their original form. They have to be processed in order to change them into more usable commodities.
Pro forma	The term pro forma is a term applied to practices that are perfunctory, pro forma earnings are those earnings of companies in addition to actual earnings calculated under the United States Generally Accepted Accounting Principles in their quarterly and yearly financial reports.
Retina	The vertebrate Retina is a light sensitive tissue lining the inner surface of the eye. The optics of the eye create an image of the visual world on the Retina, which serves much the same function as the film in a camera. Light striking the Retina initiates a cascade of chemical and electrical events that ultimately trigger nerve impulses.
Working capital	Working capital, also known as net working capital or NWC, is a financial metric which represents operating liquidity available to a business. Along with fixed assets such as plant and equipment, working capital is considered a part of operating capital. It is calculated as current assets minus current liabilities.
Risk	Risk concerns the expected value of one or more results of one or more future events. Technically, the value of those results may be positive or negative. However, general usage tends focus only on potential harm that may arise from a future event, which may accrue either from incurring a cost (`downside Risk`) or by failing to attain some benefit (`upside Risk`).
Small business	A Small business is a business that is privately owned and operated, with a small number of employees and relatively low volume of sales. The legal definition of `small` often varies by country and industry, but is generally under 100 employees in the United States and under 50 employees in the European Union. In comparison, the definition of mid-sized business by the number of employees is generally under 500 in the U.S. and 250 for the European Union.
Businesses	A business (, enterprise or firm) is a legally recognized organization designed to provide goods and/or services to consumers. Businesses are predominant in capitalist economies, most being privately owned and formed to earn profit that will increase the wealth of its owners and grow the business itself. The owners and operators of a business have as one of their main objectives the receipt or generation of a financial return in exchange for work and acceptance of risk.

Chapter 33. Entrepreneur or Intrapreneur?

Asset	In business and accounting, Assets are economic resources owned by business or company. Anything tangible or intangible that one possesses, usually considered as applicable to the payment of one`s debts is considered an Asset. Simplistically stated, Assets are things of value that can be readily converted into cash (although cash itself is also considered an Asset).
Intrapreneur	In 1992, The American Heritage Dictionary brought Intrapreneurism into the main stream by adding Intrapreneur to its dictionary, defining it as `a person within a large corporation who takes direct responsibility for turning an idea into a profitable finished product through assertive risk-taking and innovation`. Intrapreneurship was a concept here to stay. The term itself dates to the 1983 PhD dissertation by Burgelman and later defined in a 1985 book by Gifford Pinchot III, `Intrapreneuring`; a revised edition, entitled `Intrapreneuring in Action` is currently published.
Corporate culture	Corporate culture is the total sum of the values, customs, traditions and meanings that make a company unique. Corporate culture is often called `the character of an organization` since it embodies the vision of the company`s founders. The values of a Corporate culture influence the ethical standards within a corporation, as well as managerial behavior.
Management process	Management process is a process of planning and controlling the performance or execution of any type of activity, such as: · a project (project Management process) or · a process (process Management process, sometimes referred to as the process performance measurement and management system). Organization`s senior management is responsible for carrying out its Management process. ·

364

Chapter 34. Domestic or Global Hospitality Positions—or Both?

Expatriate	An Expatriate is a person temporarily or permanently residing in a country and culture other than that of the person's upbringing or legal residence. The word comes from the Latin ex (out of) and patria (country, fatherland). In its broadest sense, an Expatriate is any person living in a different country from where he is a citizen.
Globalization	Globalization (or globalisation) describes an ongoing process by which regional economies, societies, and cultures have become integrated through a globe-spanning network of communication and exchange. The term is sometimes used to refer specifically to economic Globalization: the integration of national economies into the international economy through trade, foreign direct investment, capital flows, migration, and the spread of technology. However, Globalization is usually recognized as being driven by a combination of economic, technological, sociocultural, political, and biological factors.
Adaptability	Adaptability (lat.: adaptÅ = fit, matching) is a feature of a system or of a process. This word has been put to use as a specialised term in different disciplines and in business operations. Word definitions of Adaptability as a specialised term differ little from dictionary definitions.
Sexual orientation	Sexual orientation is a pattern of emotional, romantic, and/or sexual attractions to men, women, both genders, neither gender, behaviors expressing them, and membership in a community of others who share them.` Sexual orientation is usually classified relative to the gender of the people who are found sexually attractive. Though people may use other labels, or none at all, Sexual orientation is usually discussed in terms of three categories: heterosexual, homosexual, and bisexual.
Absolute advantage	In economics, Absolute advantage refers to the ability of a party (an individual, or country) to produce more of a good or service than competitors, using the same amount of resources. If a party has an Absolute advantage when using the same input as another party, it can produce a greater output. Since Absolute advantage is determined by a simple comparison of labor productivities, it is possible for a party to have no Absolute advantage in anything.
Anecdotal value	In economics, Anecdotal value refers to the primarily social and political value of an anecdote or anecdotal evidence in promoting understanding of a social, cultural, in the last several decades the evaluation of anecdotes has received sustained academic scrutiny from economists and scholars such as S.G. Checkland (on David Ricardo), Steven Novella, Hollis Robbins, R. Charleton, Kwamena Kwansah-Aidoo, and others; these academics seek to quantify the value inherent in the deployment of anecdotes. More recently, economists studying choice models have begun assessing Anecdotal value in the context of framing; Kahneman and Tversky suggest that choice models may be contingent on stories or anecdotes that frame or influence choice.

Chapter 34. Domestic or Global Hospitality Positions—or Both?

Exchange rate	Exchange rates Currency band Exchange rate Exchange rate regime Fixed Exchange rate Floating Exchange rate Linked Exchange rate Markets effective Exchange rate · 5 Uncovered interest rate parity · 6 Asset market model · 7 Fluctuations in Exchange rates · 8 .
Business	A Business (, enterprise or firm) is a legally recognized organization designed to provide goods and/or services to consumers. Businesses are predominant in capitalist economies, most being privately owned and formed to earn profit that will increase the wealth of its owners and grow the Business itself. The owners and operators of a Business have as one of their main objectives the receipt or generation of a financial return in exchange for work and acceptance of risk.
Culture	Culture is a term that has different meanings. For example, in 1952, Alfred Kroeber and Clyde Kluckhohn compiled a list of 164 definitions of `culture` in culture: A Critical Review of Concepts and Definitions. However, the word `culture` is most commonly used in three basic senses: · Excellence of taste in the fine arts and humanities, also known as high culture · An integrated pattern of human knowledge, belief, and behavior that depends upon the capacity for symbolic thought and social learning · The set of shared attitudes, values, goals, and practices that characterizes an institution, organization or group When the concept first emerged in eighteenth- and nineteenth-century Europe, it connoted a process of cultivation or improvement, as in agriculture or horticulture. In the nineteenth century, it came to refer first to the betterment or refinement of the individual, especially through education, and then to the fulfillment of national aspirations or ideals.
Disaster	A Disaster is the tragedy of a natural or human-made hazard (a hazard is a situation which poses a level of threat to life, health, property) that negatively affects society or environment. In contemporary academia, Disasters are seen as the consequence of inappropriately managed risk. These risks are the product of hazards and vulnerability.

Chapter 34. Domestic or Global Hospitality Positions—or Both?

Culture shock	Culture shock refers to the anxiety and feelings (of surprise, disorientation, uncertainty, confusion, etc). felt when people have to operate within a different and unknown cultural or social environment, such as a foreign country. It grows out of the difficulties in assimilating the new culture, causing difficulty in knowing what is appropriate and what is not.
Time	Time is a component of the measuring system used to sequence events, to compare the durations of events and the intervals between them, and to quantify the motions of objects. Time has been a major subject of religion, philosophy, and science, but defining it in a non-controversial manner applicable to all fields of study has consistently eluded the greatest scholars. In physics and other sciences, Time is considered one of the few fundamental quantities.
Concepts	Kant declared that human minds possess pure or a priori concepts. Instead of being abstracted from individual perceptions, like empirical concepts, they originate in the mind itself. He called these concepts categories, in the sense of the word that means predicate, attribute, characteristic, or quality.
Regulation	Regulation is `controlling human or societal behaviour by rules or restrictions.` Regulation can take many forms: legal restrictions promulgated by a government authority, self-Regulation, social Regulation (e.g. norms), co-Regulation and market Regulation. One can consider Regulation as actions of conduct imposing sanctions (such as a fine). This action of administrative law, or implementing regulatory law, may be contrasted with statutory or case law.
Regulations	The Control of Substances Hazardous to Health regulations 2002 is a United Kingdom Statutory Instrument that stipulates general requirements on employers to protect employees and other persons from the hazards of substances used at work by risk assessment, control of exposure, health surveillance and incident planning. There are also duties on employees to take care of their own exposure to hazardous substances and prohibitions on the import of certain substances into the European Economic Area. The regulations reenacted with amendements the Control of Substances Hazardous to Work regulations 1999 and implement several European Union directives.
GROW model	The GROW model (or process) is a technique for problem solving or goal setting. It was developed in the UK and used extensively in the corporate coaching market in the late 1980s and 1990s. There have been many claims to authorship of GROW as a way of achieving goals and solving problems.
Selection	In the context of evolution, certain traits or alleles of a species may be subject to selection. Under selection, individuals with advantageous or `adaptive` traits tend to be more successful than their peers reproductively--meaning they contribute more offspring to the succeeding generation than others do. When these traits have a genetic basis, selection can increase the prevalence of those traits, because offspring will inherit those traits from their parents.

Chapter 34. Domestic or Global Hospitality Positions—or Both?

Chapter 34. Domestic or Global Hospitality Positions—or Both?

Selection process	The selection process for College basketball`s NCAA Men`s Division I Basketball Championship determines which 65 teams will enter the tournament and where they will be seeded and placed in the bracket. It is done by a special selection committee appointed by the NCAA. Thirty teams have automatic bids by winning their conference tournament; the Ivy League regular-season champion receives an automatic bid because the Ivy League has no conference tournament .
Employment	Employment is a contract between two parties, one being the employer and the other being the employee. An employee may be defined as: `A person in the service of another under any contract of hire, express or implied, oral or written, where the employer has the power or right to control and direct the employee in the material details of how the work is to be performed.` Black`s Law Dictionary page 471 (5th ed. 1979).
	In a commercial setting, the employer conceives of a productive activity, generally with the intention of generating a profit, and the employee contributes labour to the enterprise, usually in return for payment of wages.

372

CPSIA information can be obtained at www.ICGtesting.com

224672LV00001B/11/P